OP 26

We Were Caught Unprepared:
The 2006 Hezbollah-Israeli War

Matt M. Matthews

U.S. Army Combined Arms Center
Combat Studies Institute Press
Fort Leavenworth, Kansas

Library of Congress Cataloging-in-Publication Data

Matthews, Matt, 1959-
  We were caught unprepared : the 2006 Hezbollah-Israeli War / by Matt Matthews.
    p. cm. -- (Long war occasional paper ; 26)
  Includes bibliographical references.
  1. Lebanon War, 2006. I. Title. II. Series.

DS87.65.M38 2008
956.9204'4--dc22

2008000097

CSI Press publications cover a variety of military history topics. The views expressed in this CSI Press publication are those of the author(s) and not necessarily those of the Department of the Army or the Department of Defense. A full list of CSI Press publications, many of them available for downloading, can be found at http://usacac.army.mil/CAC/csi/RandP/CSIpubs.asp.

The seal of the Combat Studies Institute authenticates this document as an official publication of the CSI. It is prohibited to use the CSI official seal on any republication of this material without the expressed written permission of the Director of CSI.

For sale by the Superintendent of Documents, U.S. Government Printing Office
Internet: bookstore.gpo.gov Phone: toll free (866) 512-1800; DC area (202) 512-1800
Fax: (202) 512-2104 Mail: Stop IDCC, Washington, DC 20402-0001

ISBN 978-0-16-079899-3

Foreword

The Combat Studies Institute (CSI) is pleased to present Long War Series Occasional Paper 26, *We Were Caught Unprepared: The 2006 Hezbollah-Israeli War* by CSI historian Mr. Matt M. Matthews. The outcome of the war that was, at best, a stalemate for Israel has confounded military analysts throughout the world. Long considered the most professional and powerful army in the Middle East, with a history of impressive military victories against its enemies, the Israeli Defense Forces (IDF) emerged from the campaign with its enemies undefeated and its prestige severely tarnished.

Matthews's historical analysis of the war includes an examination of IDF and Hezbollah doctrine prior to the war, as well as an overview of the operational and tactical problems encountered by the IDF during the war. His research convincingly argues that the Israeli reliance on poorly understood and controversial Effects-Based Operations (EBO) and Systemic Operational Design (SOD) warfighting theories, and a nearly singular dependence on air power, were root causes of Israeli problems. Additionally, after years of counterinsurgency (COIN) operations in the Gaza Strip and West Bank territories, IDF ground forces were tactically unprepared and untrained to fight against a determined Hezbollah force that conducted what was, in many ways, a conventional, fixed-position defense. In researching this study, Mr. Matthews interviewed several prominent IDF officers and other experts in the field, many of whom had not previously been interviewed. The result is an insightful, comprehensive examination of the war.

In 2006, Hezbollah demonstrated that terrorist groups around the world are capable of learning from, adapting to, and exploiting weaknesses in conventional military forces. Inasmuch as the US Army has focused almost exclusively on irregular warfare since 2001, the lessons offered in this analysis are particularly relevant. We believe that this study will be of great use to the US Army as it conducts current operations and prepares for an uncertain future in which potential enemies are watching and learning. *CSI–The Past is Prologue!*

Timothy R. Reese
Colonel, Armor
U.S. Army Combined Arms Center
Director, Combat Studies Institute

Acknowledgments

This Long War Series Paper could not have been written without the help of numerous individuals. Dr. Gil Ariely, a Reserve major and Chief Knowledge Officer in the Israeli Defense Forces took time out of his demanding schedule to visit with me and answer a multitude of questions here at Fort Leavenworth, Kansas. Adam Harmon, author, Israeli soldier, and American citizen provided invaluable advice on the Israeli incursion into Lebanon from 1982 to 2000. Ehud Eiran, a Reserve officer in the IDF, author, and former Assistant Foreign Policy Advisor to Prime Minister Ehud Barak provided helpful information related to the 2000 Israeli withdrawal from Lebanon, as well as the assassination of Israeli Brigadier General Erez Gerstein in February of 1999. Ron Tira, author, former Israeli Air Force (IAF) fighter pilot, former section chief of the IAF intelligence division ("Lamdan") and current reservist in the IAF Campaign Planning Department responded to a host of e-mail questions and provided guidance and assistance throughout this project. Brigadier General (Retired) Shimon Naveh, former chief of the IDF's Operational Theory Research Institute (OTRI), also provided important information related to his Systemic Operational Design. I am indebted to each of them for their candor and expertise. However, any inaccuracies in this work are mine alone.

I would like to thank Mr. Kendall D. Gott, CSI Senior Historian, Research and Publications Team, for his counsel on this project, as well as the efforts of my editor Jennifer Lindsey. I would also like to acknowledge Colonel Timothy R. Reese, CSI Director, and Dr. William G. Robertson, CSI Deputy Director and Combined Arms Center (CAC) Command Historian, for their advice and support in this effort.

Finally, without the encouragement and steadfast support of my wife, Susan Day Harmison, this work might have never been completed.

Contents

Introduction

The Israelis, regulars and reservists, fought like demons. In the words of the Prophet Joel: "Their faces gathered blackness; they ran like mighty men; they climbed the wall and did not break rank; the earth quaked before them; and the Lord made His voice heard in front of His army."

Martin van Creveld
on the 1967 Six-Day War

On 12 July 2006, a well-trained, highly motivated detachment of Hezbollah* fighters crossed from southern Lebanon into northern Israel killing three Israeli soldiers and abducting two others. Israeli Prime Minister Ehud Olmert called the incursion "an act of war" and proclaimed "Lebanon will suffer the consequences of its actions."[1] Convinced they could force Hezbollah to disarm and withdraw from southern Lebanon by initiating an effects based air campaign, the Israeli Air Force (IAF) began pounding targets across Lebanon. Although initially taken aback by the destructive air strikes, Hezbollah unleashed its own attack within 24 hours, launching an extensive rocket barrage from southern Lebanon into Israel.

Despite Israel assuring the United States of a "quick and decisive" resolution to the conflict, Hezbollah's short-range Katyusha rockets continued to rain down on the Israeli population.[2] As days went by, it became increasingly apparent to both the Israeli Defense Forces (IDF) and western military analysts that the IAF was having little effect on Hezbollah's rockets.

When the IDF reluctantly moved its ground forces into southern Lebanon, the apparent ineffectiveness of the operation and the stubborn resistance of Hezbollah fighters stunned military observers worldwide. After years of highly successful counterinsurgency (COIN) operations against the Palestinians, the IDF appeared remarkably inept to conduct a successful conventional ground campaign against Hezbollah.

Without question, the Israeli ground campaign revealed an army confused by its new doctrine. Soldiers were deficient in training and equipment, and senior officers seemed woefully unprepared to fight a "real war." By the time the United Nations (UN) cease-fire went into effect on 14 August 2006, many military analysts were convinced the IDF had suffered a significant defeat. One source held that Hezbollah's military

* Throughout this text, Hezbollah and Hizbollah are used interchangeably. Hebrew translations tend to use Hizbollah instead of Hezbollah.

1

and political victory was absolute and irrefutable.[3] Even more revealing were the comments by Mossad Chief, Meir Degan, and the head of Shin Bet, Yuval Diskin, during a meeting with Prime Minister Olmert in the immediate aftermath of the war. Both men pointedly told Olmert "the war was a national catastrophe and Israel suffered a critical blow."[4]

No conflict in the recent past provides a more illuminating study for the US Army than the 2006 Hezbollah-Israeli war. After years of conducting successful counterinsurgency operations against the Palestinians, the Israeli military encountered substantial problems in shifting its focus to major combat operations against Hezbollah. As with the IDF prior to the 2006 war, the US Army, at least for the last three years, has focused almost exclusively on irregular warfare.[5] For the IDF, these operations seriously dulled ground maneuver combat skills, particularly among tank crewmen. The IDF's steadfast acceptance of a new doctrine inspired by Effects-Based Operations (EBO), Systemic Operational Design (SOD), and standoff firepower-based operations also proved problematic. Implications for the US Army in this arena should prove enlightening.

Chapter 1 of this study provides a concise history of the Israeli withdrawal from Lebanon in 2000. The chapter examines Hezbollah's guerrilla doctrine and its masterful campaign to remove the IDF from southern Lebanon. Also closely investigated is the manner by which Hezbollah turned the Israeli withdrawal into a humiliating rout. This lesson should be of particular interest to all US Army officers to ensure that any withdrawal from current US Army operations will not prove similarly problematic.

Chapter 2 offers an overview of Hezbollah's changing doctrine, as well as the buildup and planning for the 2006 war. Also examined is the IDF's reliance on its new EBO doctrine that allocated monetary resources to air power and technology at the expense of IDF ground forces. The IDF's long counterinsurgency efforts against the Palestinians and the resulting negative effects on IDF ground forces are also explored.

Chapter 3 focuses on events occurring between 12–16 July. This includes the kidnapping and killing of Israeli soldiers by Hezbollah and the resulting war, as well as the futile effects-based campaign to remove Hezbollah from southern Lebanon. The inherent miscalculations, which led to the monumental failings of the IDF's leadership, are also studied.

Chapter 4 addresses events from 17 July through 14 August. Topics covered are the failure of the IDF's ground campaign against Hezbollah, and the confusion caused by IDF doctrine, as well as the lack of training and leadership within the IDF on the ground. Also probed are problems associated with the hasty mobilization of the IDF's reserve ground forces and their lack of both training and equipment. Equally important is the analysis of Hezbollah's tactics, particularly its use of "swarming" antitank guided missiles (ATGMs) against the poorly trained IDF tank forces.

For six years, the IDF conducted a counterinsurgency campaign against the Palestinians and developed a doctrine rooted in EBO and high-tech wizardry. However, in the summer of 2006, when confronted by a conventional war with Hezbollah, the Israeli military proved incapable of defeating a minor adversary. Although research and analysis of this recent conflict are still ongoing, the emerging details of ill-conceived doctrine and an army marred by long years of counterinsurgency operations still yield valid and important lessons for today's US Army officers.

Notes

1. Jeremy M. Sharp, *Israel-Hamas-Hezbollah: The Current Conflict*, CRS Report for Congress, Congressional Research Service, The Library of Congress, 21 July 2006, 6.

2. Augustus Richard Norton, "Hezbollah: A Short History" (Princeton and Oxford: Princeton University Press, 2007), 139.

3. Alastair Crooke and Mark Perry, "How Hezbollah Defeated Israel, Part 2: Winning the Ground War," *Asia Times Online*, 13 October 2006, http://www.atimes.com/atimes/Middle_East/HJ13Ak01.html (accessed 14 February 2008).

4. "Secret Meeting," *Ynetnews.com,* 30 March 2007, http://www.ynetnews.com/Ext/Comp/ArticleLayout/CdaArticlePrintPreview/1,2506,L-3383151,00.html. Also see, Ofer Shelah and Yoav Limor, *Shvuyim belevanon: ha'emet al milkhemet levanon hashniya* (*Captives in Lebanon*) (Tel Aviv: Yedioth Books, 2007).

5. The types of military operations that fall under irregular warfare include counterinsurgency, support to an insurgency, unconventional warfare, foreign internal defense, and combating terrorism. "Army Doctrine Update," Combined Arms Doctrine Directorate, US Army Combined Arms Center, Fort Leavenworth, KS, 24 February 2007, 5.

Chapter 1

The 2000 Israeli Withdrawal from Lebanon

It was also not expected of the Resistance to concentrate its equipment and resources on the front lines and go through a classic war with the enemy, for this was an army role and required sufficient numbers, equipment and military capabilities. Resistance work was essentially "hit and run," leaving the enemy surprised without any visible retaliation targets.

Sheikh Naim Qassem
Deputy Secretary-General of Hezbollah

The pullout from Lebanon descended into chaos, as Israeli troops staggered back across the border, telling reporters that their military equipment and training had proven useless against Hezbollah, and its Lebanese allies.

Joel Himelfarb
The Washington Times

Near midday on 28 February 1999, a small convoy of vehicles passed down the narrow, dusty mountain road near the village of Kafr Shaba, in the Israeli-occupied security zone of south Lebanon. An armor-plated Mercedes driven by Chief Warrant Officer Imad Abu-Rish led the motorcade down the mountainside. Riding with Abu-Rish was his commander, Brigadier General Erez Gerstein, radio operator Staff Sergeant Omer El-Kabetz, and popular Israeli radio reporter, Ilan Roeh.[1]

At 38, Gerstein commanded all Israeli Defense Forces in southern Lebanon and was regarded as a legendary figure within the IDF, a leader impervious to harm. As Israeli support for the long, costly war in Lebanon slowly eroded, Gerstein remained firm in his convictions. "Israelis calling for a unilateral withdrawal from Lebanon," he warned, "were endangering the lives of soldiers serving there." Gerstein also suggested "that withdrawal from the security zone would bring the terror right up to Israel's borders." Resolute and confident, he was determined to defeat the IDF's most threatening enemy in Lebanon, Hezbollah (the Party of God).[2]

As the three-vehicle convoy made its way back down the treacherous mountain road to IDF headquarters in Marjayoun, Gerstein's Mercedes rounded a jagged curve. At precisely the same moment, a massive

5

improvised explosive device (IED) detonated next to the car. The explosion ripped through the Mercedes, engulfing the automobile in flames. Abu-Rish, El-Kabetz, and Roeh were blown out of the vehicle and mortally wounded as the Mercedes tumbled over a cliff with Gerstein still inside. Rescuers who raced down the precipice to save him were unable to remove their commander from the burning wreckage and watched helplessly as he burned to death. The killing of the highest ranking Israeli officer in Lebanon by Hezbollah confirmed its status as Israel's most intractable enemy.[3]

The ambush was filmed by Hezbollah and aired on all Lebanese television stations. Professor Judith Palmer Harik, a resident of Beirut, recounted, "Hezbollah was pressing home the point, that any Israeli military personnel on Lebanese soil was fair game and that even high ranking officers were not safe. . . . Lebanese friends with whom I watched the recording of this operation on the evening news expressed surprise about the pinpoint accuracy of the explosion. . . ."[4] While Gerstein's death had little effect militarily, it was nonetheless a "psychological defeat" for Israelis.[5]

By March 1999, a majority of Israelis were demanding an end to the Lebanese quagmire.[6] For over 20 years, Israel had waged an almost continual military campaign in Lebanon, first in opposition to the terrorist acts of the Palestine Liberation Organization (PLO), then against a variety of Lebanese secular groups determined to force the Israelis out of their country.

The IDF's 1982 invasion of Lebanon, named Operation PEACE FOR GALILEE, was designed to destroy the PLO threat to Israel and shatter its capacity to wage war. At the onset of the campaign, three Israeli heavy divisions hastily moved north to the outskirts of Beirut, trapping and killing numerous PLO members and driving the remnants into headlong retreat. At the same time, the Israeli Air Force (IAF) destroyed most, if not all, of the Syrian air defense systems in Lebanon without a single loss. According to Israeli author and IAF intelligence officer Ron Tira, "the PLO never recovered from 1982 and never regained its capabilities."[7]

Although the IDF defeated the PLO, it still faced a large Lebanese population who were not at all happy with the Israeli occupation. Many who had initially greeted the IDF as liberators now turned against their Israeli occupiers. Of all Israel's enemies, none proved more problematic than the Shiite faction Hezbollah. Created in response to Israel's continued occupation of Lebanon, this militia force was trained, armed, and equipped by Iran and Syria.[8]

6

Plagued by unremitting attacks spearheaded by Hezbollah and other secular groups, the IDF withdrew into southern Lebanon in 1985. In the new security zone, which encompassed 10 percent of Lebanon, the IDF and its ally, the South Lebanon Army (SLA), began constructing a string of company-size fortified outposts. Ignoring United Nations Resolution 425, which called for a complete Israeli withdrawal from Lebanon, the IDF and SLA prepared for a lengthy stay. Israel made it clear that, unless they could have some assurance against terrorist border incursions and rocket attacks from Lebanon, they would remain in the security zone.[9]

Hezbollah, however, was determined to drive the IDF out of Lebanon, believing that, unless attacks continued, the Israelis would never leave.[10] Beginning in 1985, they relentlessly assaulted the IDF and SLA in the security zone. Hezbollah developed 13 principles of war, specifically designed to defeat a relatively fixed, technologically advanced enemy.

1. Avoid the strong, attack the weak—attack and withdrawal!

2. Protecting our fighters is more important than causing enemy casualties!

3. Strike only when success is assured!

4. Surprise is essential to success. If you are spotted, you have failed!

5. Don't get into a set-piece battle. Slip away like smoke, before the enemy can drive home his advantage!

6. Attaining the goal demands patience, in order to discover the enemy's weak points!

7. Keep moving; avoid formation of a front line!

8. Keep the enemy on constant alert, at the front and in the rear!

9. The road to the great victory passes through thousands of small victories!

10. Keep up the morale of the fighters; avoid notions of the enemy's superiority!

11. The media has innumerable guns whose hits are like bullets. Use them in the battle!

12. The population is a treasure—nurture it!

13. Hurt the enemy and then stop before he abandons restraint![11]

Hezbollah's Deputy Secretary-General, Sheikh Naim Qassem, elaborated further on this asymmetrical concept in his book, *Hizbullah: The Story from Within*. He wrote that Hezbollah's doctrine helped accomplish a number of goals, two of which included:

1. Confusing the enemy and obliging its command to call for a constant state of alert, eventually leading to the exhaustion and decline in power.

2. Spreading panic among enemy troops, the fear of death persisted after every successful or possible resistance attack. This served to shake enemy morale and subsequently affected troop performance.[12]

As time would prove, the doctrine provided an exceptionally effective blueprint for victory.

By the 1990s, Hezbollah had transformed itself into a highly competent resistance organization, as well as an emergent political party with extensive support among the Lebanese population. Its principal intent, according to Professor Judith Palmer Harik:

> . . . was to stampede the Israelis and the SLA into as disorderly and as costly a withdrawal as possible by imposing casualties that further eroded the troops' morale and increased domestic pressure for their departure. Strategists therefore aimed at clever operations that would emphasize Hezbollah's implacability and long reach and demonstrate the enemy's vulnerability.[13]

Hezbollah slowly chiseled away at Israeli public support for the war by inflicting a constant stream of casualties on Israeli military forces. Suicide bombings, sophisticated ambushes, and direct attacks on the IDF and SLA were often captured on film and shown on Hezbollah's television station, al-Manar. The disturbing images were beamed into Israeli households, depicting the horrors of war often muted by Israeli television.[14]

The Israelis did not remain entirely on the defensive. In 1993, in response to increased casualties in the security zone, they launched Operation ACCOUNTABILITY. Hezbollah had prepared for an Israeli ground offensive and was taken aback by the massive Israeli air and artillery campaign waged against them. The military operation was unlike any Hezbollah had encountered in that the Israelis chiefly employed standoff-based precision firepower. It proved a valuable lesson and one that would better prepare Hezbollah for the next war.[15]

The next major clash between Hezbollah and Israel came in 1996. When Hezbollah rockets wounded 38 civilians in northern Israel, the IDF unleashed Operation GRAPES OF WRATH. Once again, the IDF generally resorted to standoff-based precision firepower or what Amir Kulick called a "fire-intense effort."[16] The new IDF campaign targeted not only Hezbollah but also civilian infrastructure targets and civilian population centers in southern Lebanon. Israel expected to cause a mass exodus of civilians from southern Lebanon, forcing the Lebanese and Syrian governments to take action against Hezbollah. Clearly, the operation was designed to force the hand of the Lebanese and Syrian governments and not to destroy Hezbollah's military capabilities.[17] Not surprisingly, Operation GRAPES OF WRATH failed miserably and served only to further alienate scores of Lebanese people and produce widespread international scorn.[18]

As Israeli precision-guided weapons and bombs rained down on southern Lebanon, Hezbollah struck back at northern Israel with hundreds of Katyusha rockets, forcing thousands of Israelis to seek cover in bomb shelters. The Hezbollah Secretary-General, Hasan Nasrallah, made it clear, "If Israel hits Lebanese civilian targets, then Hizballah hits Israel."[19] Although Israel inflicted heavy losses on Hezbollah, at no time during Operation GRAPES OF WRATH was the IDF's standoff precision weaponry able to silence Hezbollah's rockets.[20] It was a lesson noted by Hezbollah and entirely ignored by the IDF. With Hezbollah capable of responding in kind, both sides reached a tacit agreement on 26 April 1996 not to target civilians.[21]

As the war in southern Lebanon continued, mounting IDF casualties propelled antiwar groups into the political spotlight as politicians and a preponderance of the public called for a unilateral withdrawal from Lebanon. The strength of the antiwar movement compelled Ehud Barak, a candidate for Prime Minister at the time, to promise a withdrawal from Lebanon if elected. Upon his election in 1999, Barak assured the Israelis he would remove the IDF from southern Lebanon within 12 months, either bilaterally or unilaterally.[22]

Hezbollah, however, was determined to accelerate the Israeli withdrawal. It offered "leniency" to all SLA members who surrendered before the withdrawal began, while continuing its attacks on SLA and IDF outposts in the security zone. New SLA defections to Hezbollah greatly alarmed the Israelis. When the IDF shut down four forward outposts near the town of Jezzine in June 1999, SLA units began withdrawing from their outposts within the city limits. Hezbollah fighters quickly moved into the town and continued to pummel the dwindling ranks of the SLA as they moved into new positions to the south.[23]

Exceedingly concerned with preventing casualties, the IDF withdrew into a handful of fortified positions. Of the 50 outposts in the security zone, the SLA manned 42. Although these strongholds were heavily fortified, Hezbollah still inflicted numerous casualties on both the IDF and SLA. Using American-made, tube-launched, optically-tracked, wire-guided missiles (TOWs), Hezbollah sent the explosive projectiles directly through the window slits of the IDF and SLA outposts. According to Professor Augustus Richard Norton, "Most of the seven Israeli soldiers felled during January and February of this year [2000] were killed by TOWs."[24]

In January 2000, the SLA was badly shaken by the assassination of one of its key leaders. Aql Hashim was killed when Hezbollah managed to place a bomb inside his house. Once again, SLA defections picked up pace. When bilateral discussions in Geneva between Syria, Israel, and the United States fell apart in March 2000, Barak began making plans for a unilateral withdrawal from Lebanon. He announced, "by July 2000, the army will withdraw to the international border, and it is from the international border that we will defend the north of the country."[25]

With Barak's announcement that the IDF would withdraw from the security zone by July, the Israeli government assured the SLA they would be protected. The government informed them that "Israel is morally and politically committed to the safety and security of the soldiers of the South Lebanon Army and the Civil administration officials who worked alongside Israel for many years to protect the southern Lebanese population from the encroachment of terrorist organizations. . . . In this context, Israel is prepared to absorb any SLA soldiers or civil officials who choose to relocate to Israel, together with their families."[26] Although the Israelis had promised the SLA sanctuary in Israel, apparently the word never filtered down to the ranks, which left them discouraged and dispirited. Although the SLA appeared solid and capable, rumors persisted within the IDF that the readiness of the SLA was dubious.[27]

On 21 May, SLA soldiers abandoned their positions in the town of Taibe. Panicky Israeli officers in the area told the SLA, "Hezbollah was coming." The dire warning threw the security zone into near chaos. By the end of the day, an SLA Shiite brigade in the central sector of the security zone collapsed, with scores of soldiers surrendering to Hezbollah. As word of the SLA disintegration spread, southern Lebanese civilians, who years before had been removed from their villages in the security zone, began moving in large numbers toward their former homes. In many cases, the civilians were moving well ahead of Hezbollah fighters.[28]

On 22 May, the IDF ordered all SLA intelligence officials to withdraw from the security zone and move to the Israeli border. As other SLA units pulled back, they destroyed their bunkers and outposts. By the end of the day, it was readily apparent that the IDF was accelerating its withdrawal. Television audiences around the world watched in stunned disbelief at the chaotic nature of the withdrawal. The Hezbollah television station, al-Manar, captured the humiliating retreat and called on "Palestinians to follow in its path," while the Arab media painted Israel as a "paper tiger."[29]

By 23 May, the SLA had completely disintegrated. Its western brigade at Bint Jbeil was ordered to pull back to the Israeli border, while the Druze brigade in the east simply melted away. In many cases, the IDF and the SLA abandoned their military equipment. When the infamous SLA prison at Khiam was liberated that afternoon, Hezbollah's al-Manar broadcast the event live around the world.[30] At the border, chaos reigned as IDF and SLA forces moved quickly into Israel. An eyewitness reported, "Israeli troops staggered back across the border, telling reporters that their military equipment and training had proven useless against Hezbollah, and its Lebanese allies."[31]

As each outpost fell, Hezbollah planted its yellow flags atop the fortifications. Israeli citizens along the border watched as the flags waved triumphantly only a short distance from their settlements. Harik reported, "Along the border fence, crowds were already gathering to taunt and throw stones at the Israeli soldiers manning the observation towers on the other side."[32] The Israeli withdrawal from the security zone was seen as a complete fiasco.

Hezbollah set out to "stampede the Israelis and the SLA into as disorderly and as costly a withdrawal as possible."[33] In the eyes of most of the world, they succeeded. One Israeli newspaper called the last day of the withdrawal a "Day of Humiliation," while an Australian military officer, with many years of experience in Lebanon, concluded, "Israel was defeated by Hezbollah in Lebanon, forcing its withdrawal on 24 May 2000." Ultimately, the superb fighting qualities of Hezbollah, Israeli war fatigue, and uncertain allies turned the withdrawal into an embarrassing rout.[34] Within days, both sides began preparations for the inevitable second round.

11

Notes

1. "Israeli General Killed In Lebanon," *BBC Online Network, BBC News*, http://news.bbc.co.uk/1/hi/world/middle_east/287941.stm, 1-3 (accessed 14 February 2008); "Commander of IDF Lebanon-Liaison Unit Killed, Warrant Officer, Soldier and Civilian Killed in Explosion," *Israel Ministry of Foreign Affairs*, http://www.israelmfa.gov.il/MFA/Government/Communiques/1999/Com mander%20of%20IDF%20Lebanon-Liaison%20Unit%20and%20Three%20Ot, 1-2 (accessed 1 August 2007); "The Occupied Zone: An Overview," *Human Rights Watch*, http://www.hrw.org/reports/1999/lebanon/Isrlb997-02.htm, 4 (accessed 5 August 2007); "Death by the roadside," *Jerusalem Post*, 1 March 1999.

2. Ehud Eiran, telephone interview by author, 25 July 2007; "Gerstein New IDF Head In Lebanon," *Jerusalem Post*, 27 February 1998; Emanuel A. Winston, "Making Israel Bleed," *Winston Mideast Analysis & Commentary*, http://gamla. org.il/english/article/1999/march/win1.htm 4 (accessed 1 August 2007); Ehud Eiran, e-mail interview by author, 5 August 2007.

3. "The Occupied Zone," 4; "Death By The Roadside;" Ehud Eiran, e-mail interview by author, 31 July, 7 August 2007; See also, Ehud Eiran, *The Essence of Longing: General Erez Gerstein and the War in Lebanon* (Tel Aviv, Israel: Yediot Books (Hebrew), 2007).

4. Judith Palmer Harik, *Hezbollah: The Changing Face of Terrorism*, (London: I.B. Tauris, 2004), 131.

5. Simon Murden, "Understanding Israel's Long Conflict in Lebanon: The Search For An Alternative Approach to Security During the Peace Process," *British Journal of Middle Eastern Studies* Vol. 27, No. 1 (May 2000): 43.

6. Ibid., 43.

7. Martin van Creveld, *The Sword and the Olive: A Critical History of the Israeli Defense Force* (New York: Public Affairs, 1998), 289–291; Daniel Isaac Helmer, *Flipside of the COIN: Israel's Lebanese Incursion Between 1982–2000*, (Fort Leavenworth, KS: Combat Studies Institute Press, 2006), 35–41; Ron Tira, e-mail interview by author, 15 August 2007.

8. Professor Augustus Richard Norton noted that "There is little doubt that Iran and Syria were deeply involved in the creation of Hizballah." Augustus Richard Norton, "Hizballah and the Israeli Withdrawal from Southern Lebanon," *Journal of Palestine Studies* Vol. 30, No. 1 (Autumn 2000), 24.

9. Martin van Creveld, *The Sword and the Olive: A Critical History of the Israeli Defense Force*, (New York: Public Affairs, 1998,) 303; Augustus Richard Norton, *Hezbollah: A Short History* (Princeton and Oxford: Princeton University Press, 2007), 81.

10. Augustus Richard Norton, *Hezbollah: A Short History* (Princeton and Oxford: Princeton University Press, 2007), 81.

11. Ehud Ya'ari, "Hizballah: 13 Principles of Warfare," *The Jerusalem Report*, 21 March 1996, quoted in Daniel Isaac Helmer, *Flipside of the COIN: Israel's Lebanese Incursion Between 1982–2000* (Fort Leavenworth, KS: Combat Studies Institute Press, 2006), 53-54.

12. Naim Qassem, trans. by Dalia Khalil, *Hizbullah: The Story from Within* (London: SAQI, 2005), 71.

13. Harik, 130.

14. Norton, "Hizballah and the Israeli Withdrawal from Southern Lebanon," 31.

15. Amir Kulick, "Hizbollah vs. the IDF: The Operational Dimension," *Strategic Assessment,* Jaffee Center for Strategic Studies, Tel Aviv University Vol. 9, No. 3 (November 2006), 1–2.

16. Ibid, 1; "Operation Grapes of Wrath," *Ynetnews.com*, 1 August 2007, 1-2, http://www.ynetnews.com/articles/0,7340,L-3284744,00.html (accessed 10 August 2007).

17. Ron Tira stated that both the 1993 and 1996 campaigns were "standoffish and were designed to push [the] civilian population to the north thereby pressing the big bosses to do something (effects)." Ron Tira, e-mail interview by author 15 August 2007.

18. "Operation Grapes of Wrath," 1–2; Norton, *Hezbollah: A Short History*, 84–85.

19. Norton, "Hizballah and the Israeli Withdrawal from Southern Lebanon," 29.

20. "Operation Grapes of Wrath," 1.

21. Norton, "Hizballah and the Israeli Withdrawal from Southern Lebanon," 29.

22. Norton, *Hezbollah: A Short History*, 88.

23. Harik, 126–127.

24. Norton, "Hizballah and the Israeli Withdrawal from Southern Lebanon," 30; Harik, 132.

25. Norton, "Hizballah and the Israeli Withdrawal from Southern Lebanon," 31; Norton, *Hezbollah: A Short History*, 88–89; Harik, 130–131.

26. "The Israeli Withdrawal from Southern Lebanon," *Jewish Virtual Library*, 4, http://www.jewishvirtuallibrary.org/jsource/Peace/lebwith.html (accessed 1 August 2007).

27. Mordechai Nisan, "Did Israel Betray Its Lebanese Allies?" *Middle East Quarterly* (December 2000), 2.

28. Ibid, 2; Harik, 137–138.

29. Nisan, 2; Abraham Rubinovich, "Despite Ragtag Pullout From Lebanon, Israel Is No Paper Tiger," *International Herald Tribune*, 30 May 2000.

30. Nisan, 2; Harik, 138.

31. Joel Himelfarb, "Hezbollah's Deadly Record," *The Washington Times*, 16 March 2005.

32. Joel Himelfarb, "Hezbollah's Deadly Record," *The Washington Times*, 16 March 2005; Harik, 138.

33. Harik, 130.

34. Major Christopher E. Whitting, *When David Became Goliath* (Fort Leavenworth, KS: US Army Command and General Staff College, 2001), 98; Helmer, 70.

Chapter 2

Planning for the Second Lebanon War

Victory means achieving the strategic goal and not necessarily territory. I maintain that we also have to part with the concept of a land battle. We have to talk about the integrated battle and about the appropriate force activating it. Victory is a matter of consciousness. Air power effects the adversary's consciousness significantly.

Commander Dan Halutz
Israeli Air Force (IAF), 2001

The Blue Line

By June 2000, a United Nations cartographic team working with the United Nations Interim Force in Lebanon (UNIFIL) had established a new border line between Lebanon and Israel. Christened the "Blue Line," the new 79-kilometer demarcation or withdrawal boundary was fully endorsed by the UN Security Council on 18 June 2000. It concluded, "As of 16 June, Israel had withdrawn its forces from Lebanon in accordance with Security Council resolution 425." According to a UN press release, Secretary-General Kofi Annan "expressed the hope that the implementation of resolution 425 would be seen by all people of the region, especially Syrians, Palestinians and Israelis, as well as Lebanese, as an encouragement to quickly move ahead in negotiating peace treaties." Annan also pointed out that UNIFIL's highest priority was "helping the Lebanese Government and armed forces to assume their responsibilities along the border and throughout the area from which Israel had withdrawn." While certainly admirable in its intentions, Annan's peace plan was doomed from the start.[1]

Due to the convoluted power structure in Lebanon, the Lebanese central government either could not or would not commit its army to police duty in southern Lebanon. The chief spokesperson for UNIFIL, Timur Goksel, was not far off the mark when he suggested, "There were political constraints . . . and they don't want to risk the army. . . . If it goes, the country follows." Further complicating the peace process was the fact that Israel had managed under the UN-brokered resolution to retain a small portion of land (Shebaa Farms) which was located at the northern end of the Golan Heights. Many Lebanese thought the land was theirs and were outraged over Israel's continued possession of Shebaa Farms. In a speech given by Lebanon's President, Emile Lahoud, in May 2000, the Lebanese leader stated that the Israeli withdrawal from the security zone was "still not enough to realize the comprehensive peace desired. . . . Israel must return all Arab lands, including Lebanon's Shebaa Farms region."[2]

The Lebanese government was still highly suspicious of Israeli intentions and therefore reluctant to send its army into southern Lebanon and dismantle Hezbollah's war-making capabilities. Undoubtedly, Syria remained the most effectual power broker in Lebanon and did not want to see Hezbollah disarmed.[3] Iran, too, relied on Hezbollah as a proxy fighting force and would not endorse its removal from southern Lebanon.[4] Out of this aberrant political situation, Hezbollah once again stepped forward as the chief defender of Lebanon. In fact, when it came to protecting Lebanon against Israel, Hezbollah believed it could perform the task a good deal more effectively than the Lebanese army. Clearly, it was not about to dismantle its military resources. "It is public knowledge," wrote Hezbollah Deputy Secretary-General Qassem, "that the Lebanese army is much weaker than its Israeli counterpart, and an Israeli decision to invade Lebanon whether by land, sea or air would be faced by army retaliation of a limited effect that could not impede a wide-scale aggression, given the obvious imbalance in capabilities." Qassem also pointed out "Experience has clearly shown that Resolution 425, diplomatic efforts and US promises did not liberate Lebanon from a twenty-two-year occupation. Lebanon was liberated through resistance and public support for such resistance. Since we are in possession of such effective means, why would we intentionally incapacitate them? What do we fear by maintaining them? And who could guarantee a deterrence of Israel should we lose them?" With massive Iranian and Syrian support, Hezbollah began organizing its military assets for the next confrontation with Israel.[5]

Hezbollah's Preparations for the 2006 Hezbollah-Israeli War

It would appear that a major portion of Hezbollah's operational design was based on the presumption that Israel no longer had a tolerance for war and its inevitable butcher's bill. In fact, Hezbollah Secretary-General Hasan Nasrallah stated in his victory speech on 26 May 2000, in the newly liberated town of Bint Jbeil, "Israeli society is as weak as a spider web." Nasrallah was convinced that "the Israeli Achilles' heel" was "Israeli society itself." The Hezbollah Secretary-General was certain "that Israeli society is a brittle post-military society that cannot endure wars anymore and that under pressure, it can succumb to Arab aggression." Building on this premise, Hezbollah was convinced that, in any future war, Israel would rely heavily on air and artillery precision weapons and limit its use of ground forces. These operational hypotheses were based on Hezbollah's experiences in its first long war with Israel. It was confident that Israel would have no stomach for casualties in any future conflict and would conduct the majority of its operations using standoff-based firepower. Available historic evidence appears to indicate this rationale was crucial as Hezbollah began its operational and tactical planning.[6]

It was imperative that Hezbollah's combat operations penetrate well inside Israel's border and not yield to the IDF's massive precision firepower. To accomplish this task, Hezbollah formed several rocket units between 2000 and 2006. South of the Litani River, Hezbollah organized the Nasser unit, which would control a vast arsenal of 122-mm Katyusha rockets that would be used to strike within Israel. To undermine any attempt by Israel to decimate Hezbollah's firepower, missile launchers were scattered across various villages and even open areas.[7]

Hezbollah established a simple, yet effective system for firing the Katyusha rockets. Once lookouts declared the area free of Israeli aircraft, a small group moved to the launch site, set up the launcher, and quickly departed. A second group would then transport the rocket to the launch location and promptly disperse. A third small squad would then arrive at the location and prepare the rocket for firing, often using remotely controlled or timer-based mechanisms. The entire process was to take less than 28 seconds with many of the rocket squads riding bicycles to the launch location. The vast majority of the rocket systems were hidden in underground caches and bunkers built to withstand precision air and artillery strikes.[8]

A second rocket unit containing medium-range FAJR and extended-range Katyusha rockets was placed both north and south of the Litani. Most, if not all, of these rockets were to be fired from vehicle-mounted launchers. Sandwiched between the Litani River and Beirut, Hezbollah added two additional long-range rocket units containing the 610-mm Zelzal-2 and other long-range systems. By 2006, Iran and Syria had supplied Hezbollah with an astonishing 12,000 to 13,000 short-, medium-, and long-range, ground-to-ground missiles. According to some intelligence sources, Iranian elements managed the offloading of the rockets in Lebanon and trained Hezbollah in their use.[9] (For a complete listing of Hezbollah rocket systems, see Appendix B).

If war erupted, Hezbollah believed it absolutely crucial to maintain a constant barrage of rockets on Israel. Hezbollah was prepared to aim for both civilian and military targets. While the group Human Rights Watch is convinced Hezbollah fired rockets "indiscriminately" into Israel during the 2006 conflict, it would be debatable to maintain that all the attacks were purposely aimed at the civilian population.[10] It should also be noted, however, that with a Circular Error Probability (CEP) of up to 5 percent of the range, the Katyushas had to be aimed at large targets, like villages and towns. This made civilian casualties all but inevitable.[11]

In order to protect its rocket systems, it was essential for Hezbollah to delay any Israeli ground attack aimed at taking out the launch sites.

A Hezbollah authority stated:

> Alongside these three or four rocket formations was a ground array created south of the Litani based on underground tunnels and bunkers, explosives-ridden areas, and anti-tank units. This array was intended to confront ground forces to a limited extent, to stall ground incursions, and inflict as many casualties as possible, which would wear out IDF forces, slow down their progress, and allow continued rocket fire.[12]

It is worth noting, however, that some experts within the IDF believe Hezbollah's ground-fighting force was not built separately or specifically to protect the rockets and delay an IDF ground assault but were built interconnected to the rocket units.[13]

The Hezbollah fighters assigned to protect the rockets were armed and equipped with a massive array of sophisticated weaponry. Reinforced with hundreds of antitank missiles ranging from the AT-14 Kornet-E to the American-made TOW, Hezbollah's veteran military personnel (many trained in Iran and Syria) were prepared to conduct elaborate antitank ambushes. (For a complete listing of Reported Hezbollah Antitank Weapons, see Appendix C). Its fighters had trained extensively to integrate mortars and rockets into this lethal mix by presighting suspected Israeli avenues of approach and training forward observers in proper indirect fire procedures. Mines and IEDs were expertly placed throughout the southern defensive sector in order to stop Israeli mechanized forces and enable Hezbollah to mass both direct and indirect fires. A sturdy and technically advanced underground command and control (C2) system was designed to help with the expedient delivery of orders to the front.[14] Evidence also suggests that Hezbollah's military commanders planned to keep firm operational control over their rocket units, while giving more tactical leeway to their ground troops.[15]

In the logistics arena, Hezbollah stockpiled every item it would need to prosecute the war effort south of the Litani. The supplies were secreted in well-fortified bunkers and entrenchments designed to withstand blistering IDF-precision firepower.[16]

18

The defensive network built by Hezbollah and its erstwhile allies in southern Lebanon was an engineering marvel. In their highly informative, three-part article, "How Hezbollah Defeated Israel," Alastair Crooke and Mark Perry described the extraordinary defensive system and Hezbollah's adroit deception plan:

> Hezbollah's robust and hardened defenses were the result of six years of diligent work, beginning with the Israeli withdrawal from the region in 2000. Many of the command bunkers designed and built by Hezbollah engineers were fortified, and a few were even air-conditioned. The digging of the arsenals over the previous years had been accompanied by a program of deception, with some bunkers being constructed in the open and often under the eyes of Israeli drone vehicles or under the observation of Lebanese citizens with close ties to the Israelis. With few exceptions, these bunkers were decoys. The building of other bunkers went forward in areas kept hidden from the Lebanese population. The most important command bunkers and weapons-arsenal bunkers were dug deeply into Lebanon's rocky hills—to a depth of 40 meters. Nearly 600 separate ammunition and weapons bunkers were strategically placed in the region south of the Litani. For security reasons, no single commander knew the location of each bunker and each distinct Hezbollah militia unit was assigned access to three bunkers only—a primary munitions bunker and two reserve bunkers, in case the primary bunker was destroyed. Separate primary and backup marshaling points were also designated for the distinct combat units, which were tasked to arm and fight within specific combat areas. The security protocols for the marshaling of troops was diligently maintained. No single Hezbollah member had knowledge of the militia's entire bunker structure.[17]

Although the Israeli intelligence community believed Hezbollah's defensive network was based on "Iranian military doctrine," another source suggests the elaborate system was based on "a defensive guerilla force organized along North Korean lines." In fact, the same source concluded that "all the movement's underground facilities, including arms dumps, food stocks, dispensaries for the wounded, were put in place primarily in 2003–2004 under the supervision of North Korean instructors." Evidence further suggests that the Iranian Revolutionary Guard was also heavily

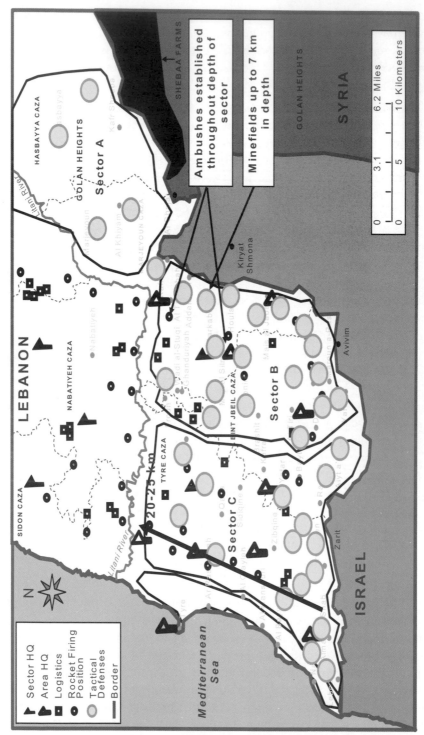

Map 1. Hezbollah Defensive System in Southern Lebanon

involved in the construction effort.[18] Intelligence sources concluded that Hezbollah was "believed to be benefiting from assistance provided by North Korean advisers, according to a July 29 report in *al-Sharq al-Awsat*. The report quotes a high-ranking Iranian Revolutionary Guard officer, who stated that North Korean advisers had assisted Hezbollah in building tunnel infrastructure, including a 25-kilometer underground tunnel."[19]

Between 2000 and 2006, Hezbollah also purportedly mastered the delicate art of counter-signals intelligence (C-SIGNET), a capability that would pay huge dividends in future wars with Israel. In the human intelligence (HUMINT) arena, Hezbollah also proved highly successful. Working with Lebanese intelligence officers, Hezbollah managed to "turn" Israeli agents in southern Lebanon and dismantle a sizable Israeli spy ring. "In some small number of crucially important cases," wrote Crooke and Perry, "Hezbollah senior intelligence officials were able to 'feed back' false information on their militia's most important emplacements to Israel with the result that Israel target folders identified key emplacements that —did not, in fact, exist."[20] It also appears likely that Hezbollah succeeded in placing its own agents in northern Israel.[21]

By the summer of 2006, Hezbollah had assembled a well-trained, well-armed, highly motivated, and highly evolved warfighting machine on Israel's northern border. Hezbollah calculated accurately and designed an organization and operational plan based on well-grounded assumptions. As reserve IAF campaign-planning officer Ron Tira pointed out, "Hizbollah designed a war in which presumably Israel could only choose which soft underbelly to expose: the one whereby it avoids a ground operation and exposes its home front vulnerability, or the one whereby it enters Lebanon and sustains the loss of soldiers in ongoing ground-based attrition with a guerilla organization. Hezbollah's brilliant trap apparently left Israel with two undesirable options."[22] At the tactical level, Hezbollah addressed the IDF's precision weapons capability by reducing its own weapon signature and target-appearance time and then building hardened defensive positions. Knowing full well that the IDF desired to "generate effects" on its "systems," Hezbollah "created a network of autonomous cells with little inter-cell systemic interaction." On the strategic level, Hezbollah also predicted that the IDF would attack with long-range precision weapons on its strategic centers of gravity (SCOG). To counter this, Hezbollah simply did away with them. In any future war with Israel, there would be no critical strategic asset to attack.[23]

The key to defeating Israel required Hezbollah to modify its doctrine. By the early summer of 2006, Hezbollah had transformed its original 13 principles of warfare (a doctrine that had worked brilliantly during the course of the Israeli occupation of Lebanon) into a new and unique design. As Hezbollah's Secretary-General Nasrallah would later point out, "The resistance withstood the attack and fought back. It did not wage a guerrilla war either . . . it was not a regular army but was not a guerrilla in the traditional sense either. It was something in between. This is the new model."[24]

It could be argued that Hezbollah's "new model," which combined both guerrilla and conventional methods, in many ways mirrored the approach adopted by the North Vietnamese and Viet Cong during their long war with the United States. In fact, one source suggests that "Hezbollah leaders studied the historical model of the Viet Cong as inspiration for establishing an advanced tunnel network, extending through the main avenues of approach into southern Lebanon."[25]

Over the course of six years, Hezbollah was able to efficiently adjust its tactics and operational design. Its planning was simple and inspired. During this time, the Israelis also formulated a new doctrine. Unfortunately for Israel, this new doctrine was highly complex and would ultimately play into the hands of Hezbollah.

Israeli Preparations for the 2006 Hezbollah-Israeli War

Within months of the IDF's withdrawal from Lebanon in 2000, Israel faced a Palestinian uprising in the West Bank and Gaza Strip. Known as the Second Intifada, the insurrection produced a massive strain on the Israeli military, particularly the ground forces. As a result of the Second Intifada, fewer recruits received suitable training, resulting a combat force often ill-prepared for the challenges ahead. The Palestinian revolt also had a deleterious effect on officers who had little experience with military operations, other than counterinsurgency warfare.[26]

During this same timeframe, Israel also continued to deal with a fairly constant stream of Hezbollah provocation on its northern border. (For a complete listing, see Appendix D). However, unlike its massive response to the Palestinian uprising, Israel, for the most part, remained reluctant to conduct any extensive retaliation against Hezbollah.[27] Many individuals in Israel contend that Prime Minister Ehud Barak certainly did not want to intensify actions against Hezbollah, as this would equate to acknowledging he was wrong in withdrawing from southern Lebanon in the first place. Prime Minister Ariel Sharon, who replaced Barak, had been driven out of politics for his role in the 1982 invasion of Lebanon. After nearly 20 years in the political wilderness, he had no intention of involving Israel in another war there.[28]

The partial findings of the Winograd Report, commissioned by the State of Israel after the 2006 war, concluded that:

> Some of the political and military elites in Israel have reached the conclusion that Israel is beyond the era of wars. It had enough military might and superiority to deter others from declaring war against her; these would also be sufficient to send a painful reminder to anyone who seemed to be undeterred; since Israel did not intend to initiate war, the conclusion was that the main challenge facing the land forces would be low intensity asymmetrical conflicts. Given these assumptions, the IDF did not need to prepare for "real war". . . .[29]

In fact, in the years following its withdrawal from southern Lebanon, the IDF began to embrace the theories of precision firepower, Effects-Based Operations (EBO), and Systemic Operational Design (SOD). EBO emerged out of the Network-Centric Warfare (NCW) concept in 2001, with the publication of a white paper by the US Joint Forces Command (JFCOM). At its core, EBO is designed to affect "the cognitive domain" of the enemy and his systems, rather than annihilating his forces.[30]

Effects-Based Operations are part of an amorphous body of thought that emerged from US Air Force doctrinal work, think tank studies, and the US Joint Forces Command in the 1990s. EBO has its roots in belief that the advent of the information age and of precision-guided munitions would allow a military force to destroy specific portions of its enemy with incredible precision. Furthermore, EBO theory held that the target of these attacks ought not to be traditional front-line ground or air forces but, instead, should be key command and control, logistics, radars, transportation, and related capabilities whose destruction will render the enemy incapable of employing his military forces and unable to accomplish his military objectives. An important secondary benefit often cited by these thinkers was the reduction in military casualties and collateral damage by the accuracy of new weapons and the avoidance of extensive ground battles.[31]

USAF theorist, John A. Warden, a leading advocate of precision firepower, divided an enemy into five concentric rings of systems with leadership at the center and fielded military forces at the outer edge. He held that precisely targeted air strikes could destroy key nodes and capabilities within the inner rings of the enemy's systems, rendering the enemy incapable of organized resistance.[32] US Air Force doctrine in 2001 stated that "precision engagement creates the opportunity for a different approach to harnessing military power to policy objectives."[33] The same doctrine used the concept of "strategic attack" to describe "operations intended to directly achieve strategic effects . . . and to achieve their objectives without first having to necessarily engage the adversary's fielded military forces in extended operations at the operational and tactical levels of war."[34] Strategists at the US Joint Forces Command used the term rapid decisive operations (RDO) to describe a new concept of war. RDO combines Effects-Based Operations "with superior knowledge and command and control capabilities" to render an enemy incoherent, thereby forcing him to "cease actions that are against US interests or have his capabilities defeated."[35]

Proponents of EBO and other theorists buttressed their claims by citing what they believed to be the dominant role of air power in the Iraq War of 1990–91 and in the Bosnian and Kosovo campaigns of the mid- and late-1990s. In 1992, for example, US Air Force historian Richard P. Hallion opined, "Simply stated, airpower won the Gulf war. In the airpower era, neither armies nor navies can be considered the primary instrument of securing victory in war."[36] Later in the decade, the famed British military historian John Keegan declared that, when the history of the Kosovo War was written, "it will, I believe, tell a quite simple story: how, for the first time in military history, air forces won a war."[37] Although they differed in the particulars, EBO proponents and other theorists generally agreed that, in the late 20th century and into the 21st, it would be possible for nations to use precision firepower, delivered primarily from the air, to destroy discrete targets within an enemy's leadership and C2 systems, and that doing so would then make it possible to achieve one's strategic objectives without the need to resort to traditional ground operations focused on the destruction of the enemy's main forces or the need to capture and hold territory.

EBO proponents within the IDF came to believe that an enemy could be completely immobilized by precision air attacks against critical military systems. The Israeli supporters of EBO also hypothesized that little or no land forces would be required since it would not be necessary to destroy the enemy.

Unlike EBO, Brigadier General Shimon Naveh's Systemic Operational Design (SOD) was a tool intended to help IDF commanders plan their campaigns. Naveh founded the IDF's Operational Theory Research Institute (OTRI) in 1995. After years of work by Naveh and other intellectuals within the OTRI, SOD attempted to provide commanders with the aptitude necessary "to think critically, systemically and methodologically about war fighting." The design focused "on the concept of the 'enemy' and provides operational commanders with tools to conceptualize both their enemies and themselves for the purpose of designing suitable campaigns," wrote a former OTRI member.[38]

Canadian Army officer L. Craig Dalton, who interviewed Naveh in 2006, described SOD as an "intellectual exercise that draws on the creative vision, experience, intuition, and judgment of commanders to provide a framework for the development of detailed operational plans."[39] For this new design, Naveh drew heavily on terminology from "post modern French philosophy, literary theory, architecture and psychology." An IDF general explained SOD in the following way:

> This space that you look at, this room that you look at, is nothing but your interpretation of it. Now, you can stretch the boundaries of your interpretation, but not in an unlimited fashion, after all, it must be bound by physics, as it contains buildings and alleys. The question is, how do you interpret the alley? Do you interpret the alley as a place, like every architect and every town planner does, to walk through, or do you interpret the alley as a place forbidden to walk through? This depends only on interpretation. We interpreted the alley as a place forbidden to walk through, and the window as a place forbidden to look through, because a weapon awaits us in the alley, and a booby trap awaits us behind the doors. This is because the enemy interprets space in a traditional, classical manner, and I do not want to obey this interpretation and fall into his trap. Not only do I not want to fall into his traps, I want to surprise him! This is the essence of war. I need to win. I need to emerge from an unexpected place. . . . This is why we opted for the methodology of moving through walls. . . . Like a worm that eats its way forward, emerging at points and then disappearing.[40]

For the IDF, the major problem with SOD was the new terminology and methodology. Not every officer in the IDF had the time or the inclination to study postmodern French philosophy. It was questionable whether the majority of IDF officers would grasp a design that Naveh proclaimed was "not intended for ordinary mortals."[41] Many IDF officers thought the entire program elitist, while others could not understand why the old system of simple orders and terminology was being replaced by a design that few could understand.[42]

After several alterations and revisions, the new IDF doctrine was endorsed and signed by the new Chief of the IDF General Staff, Lieutenant-General Dan Halutz, in April 2006. Halutz was the first IAF officer ever appointed Chief of the IDF General Staff. On the first page of the document, Halutz wrote, "Familiarity with and use of the concept of operation are the key to our success in warfare, in which the only option available is victory. Therefore, the commanding officers of the IDF must understand, assimilate and implement what is written there when they call their forces into action and prepare them for their goal."[43] It is possible that not even Halutz understood the new doctrine he endorsed and signed. Naveh explained that the "core of this document is the theory of SOD." However, Naveh remains convinced that Halutz failed to link SOD with other elements and harshly criticized his military acumen.[44]

According to Ron Tira, the new doctrine was designed to cover "strategy, force transformation, EBO as well as introducing a new military language and new structure for staff work methodology, battlefield analysis and orders structure and contents. While it is not exactly based on Shimon Naveh's SOD," Tira noted, "it is very much inspired by it" and "the borders between EBO and SOD were blurred in this doctrine."

Tira also pointed out that:

> Similar to SOD, it replaces the "old" structure of Mission, Commander's Intent, Forces and Tasks . . . with a whole new world of Political Directive, Strategic Purpose, System Boundaries, operational Boundaries, Campaign's Organizing Theme, Opposite System Rationale . . . and so on. Field commanders did not like the new doctrine, principally because they didn't understand it. Of the 170 pages long doctrine document, many experienced officers didn't understand more than half. Officers responsible for planning EBOs in the Air Force, could not understand the definition of EBO (more precisely in Hebrew Effect-Based Campaigns) or of the definition of the word "Campaign" in the document. The terminology used was too complicated, vain, and could not be understood by the thousands of officers that needed to carry it out. . . . The new terminology and methodology was supposed to be limited to the higher levels of command, and at the level of theater command and definitely at the division level, the old terminology and methodology should have been used. Nonetheless, it trickled down. . . . Commanders

need to speak in a simple accessible manner, composed essentially of two things: what do we occupy and what do we blow up. This is understandable. When an order is given to render the enemy "incoherent" or to make the enemy feel "distress" or "chased down," or to "achieve standoff domination of the theatre" field commanders simply do not know what to do and cannot judge how well or how bad they are progressing.[45]

By the spring of 2006, the problematic new doctrine was in place, but few IDF officers were willing to step forward and voice their concerns. One astute observer noted these officers were convinced "that the tailors were selling nonsense, that there were no new clothes, but were too embarrassed to say so out loud. They thought they were not smart enough. Until the war came and pointed at the king's [nakedness]."[46]

Even before Halutz took command, the IDF was stretched to the limit by budgetary cuts to the ground forces and the continuing demands placed on them by the Palestinian uprising. To make matters worse, soldiers with perishable combat skills, such as tank crewmen, patrolled the West Bank and Gaza Strip, in some cases, going years without training on their armored vehicles. A distraught reserve armored battalion commander condemned the three IDF chiefs of staff before Halutz "for having neglected the land forces in favor of the air force, for sacrificing ground mobility on the altar of high-tech wizardry, and for squandering tank specialists in the nooks and crannies of the intifada." He also pointed out that prior to the outbreak of war in the summer of 2006, reservist tank crews received little training. "To be in top form," he stated, "a tank reservist needs a five-day refresher exercise each year. Most hardly got that in the course of three years, others in the space of five, and yet others none at all."[47]

The IDF also made sizable cuts in the reserve ground forces' budget and equipment. According to the Winograd Report, "the quality of the equipment in the depots sent a message about values to the reserve soldiers. And in fact, missing, obsolete or broken equipment told the reservist that there was no one making sure that he would be equipped in a manner . . . that would allow him to operate in an optimal way . . . when he was called to the flag."[48]

Even more disturbing than the reserves cuts and the breakdown of skills at the tactical level was the fact that many high-ranking IDF officers, both regular and reserve, had not received adequate training. "Brigade generals were under-trained, and commanders above brigade level did not command their units in training for years," Tira wrote. "Some reserve units did not train in large formations for 4-6 years. What is interesting here is that this under-training was not the result of neglect or omission, but of intentional policy."

Under the IDF's new doctrine, the corps formation was eliminated, and plans were in the works to also abolish the division when the war erupted in 2006. According to Tira, Halutz and the followers of Naveh's SOD "did not see a role for land formations larger than a brigade." Brigadier generals were to command an element that when translated from Hebrew means "Campaign Trend" or "Operational Trend." These elements would be responsible for implementing "a specific effect in the framework of the EBO. Each brigadier general would command a Campaign Trend to realize an effect, and all of them together should have constituted the EBO. A Campaign Trend was not an organic unit and the brigadier general should have been given the different elements or 'molecules' (brigades, air power, special operations, etc.) necessary for generating the effect. . . . The important point is that they did not see training above brigade level as important and therefore did not invest in it." Tira also concluded that the new doctrine inflated the "focus on the cognitive side of war and the media war. Instead of killing the bad guys like in the good old days, they wanted to create a 'consciousness of victory' on our side and 'cognitive perception of defeat' on the other side."[49]

By early summer 2006, the IDF had been highly successful in its low-intensity campaign against the Palestinians. Having managed to dismantle the terrorist infrastructure in 2002, the IDF spent the next four years conducting irregular operations, detaining new terrorist recruits, and keeping a tight lid on the volatile situation. However, budget cuts and constant patrolling of Palestinian areas had greatly reduced the combat proficiency of IDF soldiers, particularly among tank crewmen.

With its overreliance on EBO, SOD, and precision firepower, the new complicated and convoluted doctrine added to the problems within the IDF. Many officers could not comprehend the doctrine while others believed it to be utter nonsense. Incredibly, a few generals brought the terminology and methodology to their divisions, divisions that had not conducted large-scale training exercises with their brigades in years.[50] Against this backdrop, Halutz remained supremely confident that the IDF could defeat any enemy who had the audacity to attack Israel.

Countdown to War

While Hezbollah Secretary-General Nasrallah had no intention of attacking Israel, he was exceedingly interested in kidnapping a few IDF soldiers. For years, Hezbollah had attempted to carry out Nasrallah's *wa'd al-sadiq* (faithful promise) to liberate Lebanese fighters still held in Israeli jails. In 2005, an attempt to capture Israeli soldiers near the town of Rajar was stopped cold by the IDF. The attack served only to intensify the already stringent Israeli security measures.

Hezbollah, however, remained undeterred and continued to plan and observe IDF forces along the border. In May 2006, conceivably in an attempt to assess the Israeli response, Hezbollah engaged an IDF outpost along the border with indirect fire, wounding one soldier. The Israeli response to the attack was quick and forceful. Using its artillery positioned close to the border, the IDF conducted pinpoint artillery strikes on 20 Hezbollah positions in southern Lebanon, reducing many of them to rubble. In response, Hezbollah fired eight Katyusha rockets at the IDF's northern command center. A former UN military observer in southern Lebanon, reported that "five of these notoriously inaccurate rockets actually hit an antennae farm near the headquarters and sent a clear reminder to Israel of the nature of Hezbollah's arsenal. . . . Both sides were clearly itching for a fight."[51] Whether or not both sides were "itching" for a full-scale war is debatable. However, by early July 2006, Hezbollah was prepared to make another attempt to kidnap IDF soldiers. This time, Hezbollah's planning was precise and meticulous, leaving nothing to chance.

Notes

1.   "United Nations Interim Force in Lebanon—Background," Peace and Security Section of the Department of Public Information in Cooperation with the Department of Peacekeeping Operations, United Nations, 2006, 1–3. http://www.un.org/Depts/dpko/missions/unifil/background.html (accessed 22 August 2007); "Press Release SC/6878." United Nations, 1 http://www.un.org/News/Press/docs/2000/20000618.sc6878.doc.html (accessed 22 August 2007).

2.   Howard Schneider, "Israel's Army Is Gone, So Where Is Lebanon's?" *The Washington Post*, 8 June 2000; Judith Palmer Harik, *Hezbollah: The Changing Face of Terrorism* (London: I.B. Tauris, 2004), 139.

3.   Norton, *Hezbollah: A Short History*, 127.

4.   Andrew Exum, "Hizballah: A Military Assessment," 7.

5.   Naim Qassem, Hizbullah: The Story from Within (London: SAQI, 2005), 133–134.

6.   Amir Kulick, "Hizbollah vs. the IDF: The Operational Dimension," *Strategic Assessment*, Jaffee Center for Strategic Studies, Tel Aviv University Vol. 9, No. 3 (November 2006), 2, http://www.tau.ac.il/jcss/sa/v9n3p7Kulick.html (accessed 15 July 2007), Sergio Catignani, "The Israeli-Hezbollah Rocket War: A Preliminary Assessment," Global Strategy Forum, September 2006, 1. www.globalstrategyforum.org (accessed 1 August 2007).

7.   Kulick, 3.

8.   "The Hezbollah Challenge… An Alternate Paradigm?" Assistant Deputy Chief of Staff for Intelligence, US Army Training and Doctrine Command, Fort Monroe, VA, No Date; Ron Tira, e-mail interview by author, 23 September 2007.

9.   Kulick, 3; Andrew Exum, "Hizbollah at War: A Military Assessment," The Washington Institute for Near East Policy, Policy Focus No. 63 (December 2006, 6); "The Hezbollah Challenge… An Alternate Paradigm?"; `"Hezbollah As A Strategic Arm Of Iran." Intelligence and Terrorism Center at the Center for Special Studies (C.S.S.), 8 September 2006, http://www.terrorism-info.org.il/site/html/search.asp?sid=13&pid=161&numResults=4&isSearch=yes&isT8=yes (accessed 21 August 2007); "Hezbollah a North Korea-Type Guerilla Force," Intelligence Online, 25 August– 7 September 2006, www.IntelligenceOnline.com (accessed 21 August 2007).

10.   "Lebanon/Israel: Hezbollah Targeted Civilians in 2006 War," Human Rights Watch, 29 August 2007, http://hrw.org/english/docs/2007/08/30/lebano16740_txt.htm (accessed 15 November 2007); Nicholas Noe, "A Response to Andrew Exum's 'Hizbollah at War: A Military Assessment,'" 5, http://64.233.167.104/search?q=cache:CYqBLHuWCV8J:www.mideastwire.com/downloads/Response%2520to%2520Andrew%2520Exum.pdf+%22a+response+to+andrew+exum%27s+%22Hizbollah+at+war&hl=en&ct=clnk&cd=1&gl=us (accessed 21 August 2006).

11.   Ron Tira, e-mail interview by author, 23 September 2007.

12.   Kulick, 3.

13. Ron Tira, e-mail interview by author, 23 September 2007.

14. "The Hezbollah Challenge... An Alternate Paradigm?"; Kulick, 4.

15. Kulick, 4.

16. David Makovsky and Jeffrey White, "Lessons and Implications of the Israel-Hizballah War: A Preliminary Assessment," *The Washington Institute for Near East Policy*, Policy Focus No. 60, October 2006, 49.

17. Alastair Crooke and Mark Perry, "How Hezbollah Defeated Israel, Part 1: Winning the Intelligence War," *Asia Times Online*, 2006, 4 http://www.atimes. com/atimes/Middle_East/HJ12AK01.html (accessed 29 June 2007).

18. "Hezbollah As A Strategic Arm of Iran." *Intelligence and Terrorism Information Center at the Center for Special Studies (C.S.S.)* 8 September 2006, 10, *http://www.terrorism-info.org.il/site/html/search.asp?sid=13&pid=161&nu mResults=4&isSearch=yes&isT8=yes* (accessed 21 August 2007); "Hezbollah a North Korea-Type Guerilla Force," *Intelligence Online*, 25 August–7 September 2006, www.IntelligenceOnline.com (accessed 21 August 2007).

19. "North Koreans Assisted Hezbollah with Tunnel Construction," *Terrorism Focus*, Vol. 3, Issue 30 (1 August 2006), 1.

20. Crooke and Perry, "Winning the Intelligence War," 7.

21. Kulick, 4-5.

22. Ron Tira, "Breaking the Amoeba's Bones," *Strategic Assessment*, Vol. 9, No. 3 (November 2006) http://www.tau.ac.il/jcss/sa/v9n3p3Tira.html (accessed 15 June 2007).

23. Ron Tira, e-mail interview by author, 22 September 2007.

24. Maryam al-Bassam, "Interview with Lebanese Hizbollah Leader Hasan Nasrallah," Beirut New TV Channel in Arabic, date of interview unknown, aired 27 August 2006, quoted in Captain Daniel Helmer, "Not Quite Counterinsurgency: A Cautionary Tale for the US Forces Based on Israel's Operation Change of Direction," *Armor* (January–February 2007), 8.

25. Helmer, 8.

26. Uri Bar-Joseph, "Their Most Humiliating Hour," *Ha'aretz*, 27 April 2007. It should be noted that this argument is rejected by some Israeli officers, who point out that prior to the 1967 war Israeli tank crewman also lacked training.

27. Zaki Shalom and Yoaz Hendel, "Conceptual Flaws on the Road to the Second Lebanon War," *Strategic Assessment*, Vol. 10, No. 1 (June 2007), 2.

28. Ron Tira, e-mail interview by author, 21 September 2007.

29. "The Winograd Report: The Main Findings of the Winograd Partial Report on the Second Lebanon War," *Haaretz.com*, 7, http://www.haaretz.com/ hasen/spages/854051.html

30. Edward A. Smith, *Effects Based Operations: Applying Network Centric Warfare in Peace, Crisis, and War* (Washington DC: The Command and Control Research Program, 2002), xv.

31. This discussion EBO relies upon an article by Timothy R. Reese, "Precision Firepower: Smart Bombs, Dumb Strategy," *Military Review*, July–August 2003, 46–53. Used with the author's permission.

32. John A. Warden, "The Enemy as a System," *Airpower Journal*, 9 (Spring 1995), 41–55.

33. US Department of the Air Force, AFDD 1, *Air Force Basic Doctrine*, (Washington, DC: US Department of the Air Force, September 1997), 30. See also, Air Force Doctrine Document 2, *Organization and Employment of Aerospace Power* (Washington, DC: US Department of the Air Force, 17 February 2000), Chap 1.

34. Ibid, 51.

35. Jeffrey J. Becker, "Rapid Decisive Operations as Joint Operational Concept," *Army* 2 (February 2002), 50. For the base RDO document, see US Joint Forces Command, *A Concept for Rapid Decisive Operations, Final Draft*, (Norfolk, VA: US Joint Forces Command, 25 October 2001).

36. Richard P. Hallion, *Storm Over Iraq: Air Power and the Gulf War* (Washington, DC; Smithsonian Institute Press, 1992), 254.

37. John Keegan, *London Daily Telegraph*, 6 June 1999.

38. Caroline Glick, "Column One: Halutz's Stalinist Moment," *The Jerusalem Post Online Edition*, 8 June 2006, http://www.jpost.com/servlet/Satelli te?cid=1149572645512&pagename=JPost%2FJPArticle%2FShowFull (accessed 12 November 2007).

39. LTC L. Craig Dalton, "Systemic Operational Design: Epistemological Bumpf or the Way Ahead for Operational Design?" A Monograph, School of Advanced Military Studies, US Army Command and General Staff College, Fort Leavenworth, KS, AY 05-06, iii.

40. Yotam Feldman, "Dr. Naveh, Or, How I Learned To Stop Worrying and Walk Through Walls," *www.haaretz.com*, 27 October 2007, http://www.haaretz. com/hasen/spages/917158.html (accessed 5 November 2007).

41. Feldman, "Dr. Neveh, Or, How I Learned To Stop Worrying and Walk Through Walls."

42. Ron Tira, e-mail interview by author, 2 November 2007.

43. Alex Fishman, "Struck by a Virus," *Yedioth Ahronoth*, B4, (No Date)

44. Shimon Naveh, interview by author, 1 November 2007.

45. Ron Tira, e-mail interview by author, 19 June 2007.

46. Alex Fishman, B4.

47. Yehuda Avner, "A Battalion Commander's Anger," *Jerusalem Post Online Edition*, 22 August 2006, http://www.jpost.com/servlet/Satellite?page name=JPost%2FJPArticle%2FShowFull&cid=1154525926212 (accessed 10 September 2007).

48. Haninah Levine, "'The Revolution in Military Affairs' Shocks but Does Not Awe Israeli Commission." *Center For Defense Information, Straus Military Reform Project*, 11 June 2007, 8.

49. Ron Tira, e-mail interview by author, 21 June 2007.

50. Ron Tira, e-mail interview by author, 19 June 2007.

51. Augustus Richard Norton, *Hezbollah: A Short History*, (Princeton and Oxford: Princeton University Press, 2007), 134-135.

Chapter 3

Opening Moves
12 July to 16 July

When a Katyusha falls on somebody's house, it's hard to
tell them this is going well.

LT Itamar Abo
Israeli Defense Forces

The Hezbollah fighter wakes up in the morning, drinks
his coffee, takes a rocket out of his closet, goes to his
neighbor's yard, sticks a clock timer on it, goes back
home and then watches CNN to see where it lands.

LTC Ishai Efroni
Deputy Commander, Baram Brigade

The Kidnapping

On 27 June 2006, the IDF issued a high alert along a portion of the border
known as milepost 105 near the village of Zarit, Israel. At this location,
the road dipped down into a low wadi or valley, making it impossible for
nearby observation posts and dug-in tanks to see IDF-mounted patrols as
they made their rounds. Certain Hezbollah had something in the works,
Israeli intelligence placed an elite Egoz reconnaissance unit in ambush
positions at milepost 105 on 27 June. For days, the Egoz team waited
to ensnare any Hezbollah fighters who might attempt to slip across the
border. By 2 July, however, no incursion materialized and the Egoz team
withdrew from the area. On that same day, the alert level was lowered to
"heightened" and, on 10 July, was reduced to just above "normal." The
IDF reserve soldiers in the vicinity of milepost 105 returned to routine
patrol duties and looked forward to the end of their reserve obligation on
12 July 2006.[1] This reserve battalion was part of Brigade 300, Division 91,
commanded by Brigadier General Gal Hirsch. Interestingly, the division
commander had warned the Israeli Defense Forces General Staff that
the "reserve battalion was not fit to operate along the northern border"
and demanded they be replaced with trained soldiers. The General Staff
rejected his request.[2]

On the night of 11 July, IDF monitors picked up several reports of
contact along the electronic border fence near milepost 105. Shortly after
these movement reports, an IDF reserve patrol reported 20 Hezbollah
fighters near the same location. Amazingly, it appears this information
never filtered down to the reserve soldiers preparing to conduct the day
patrol in the milepost 105 sector.[3]

At 0845, 12 July, the reserve soldiers assembled for their last patrol of the milepost 105 sector. Reports indicate a festive atmosphere that morning. In violation of IDF standing operating procedure (SOP), the squad conducted no briefing, prepatrol exercise or inspection and did not wait to be dispatched by their dispatching officer. As the soldiers loaded onto two high-mobility multipurpose wheeled vehicles (HMMWVs), they pitched their civilian luggage into the vehicles, intent on going directly home once they completed their patrol.[4]

At 0855, as the two HMMWVs arrived at milepost 105, an observation tower spotted a Hezbollah fighter armed with an antitank missile hiding in the weeds nearby. The observation tower was apparently unable to relay this information to the patrol. The reserve soldiers once again violated their SOP by not dismounting a team from their HMMWVs and moving tactically toward the low point in the road. Instead, no one dismounted, and both vehicles moved close together (in violation of SOP) toward milepost 105. At precisely 0900, as the two HMMWVs rolled forward, an IED exploded next to the two vehicles. At the same time, several antitank missiles slammed into the HMMWVs, killing three soldiers and wounding four others.[5] As the vehicles exploded and burned, Hezbollah fighters ran forward pulling two of the wounded soldiers from the burning wreckage. Placing the IDF soldiers on their backs, the Hezbollah fighters moved quickly back across the border.[6] In an effort to mask their attack and cause confusion within the IDF border command, Hezbollah opened fire on IDF locations and Israeli villages along the milepost 105 sector with mortars, rockets, antitank missiles, and snipers.[7]

The situation was so chaotic that the IDF battalion commander responsible for the area did not realize until 0927 that Hezbollah had abducted two of his soldiers. Once the situation became clear, he promptly broadcast the code word HANNIBAL to all IDF forces in the Northern Command, indicating an Israeli soldier had been kidnapped. Ideally, the issuing of this code word would have set in motion a chain of preplanned events designed to rescue kidnapped IDF soldiers.[8]

Upon issuing the code word, the battalion commander was to move his forces rapidly into Lebanon and attempt to cut off Hezbollah's escape routes. Unfortunately for the kidnapped soldiers, this movement never materialized. Concerned with mines and IEDs, he chose not to advance. By 0933, however, certain portions of HANNIBAL were put into motion. "Automatic" artillery fire onto Hezbollah positions went forward as planned but was "executed only partially and with long delays." By 0939, IDF attack helicopters arrived at milepost 105 where they found the smoldering wreckage of the HMMWVs but no sign of Hezbollah fighters.

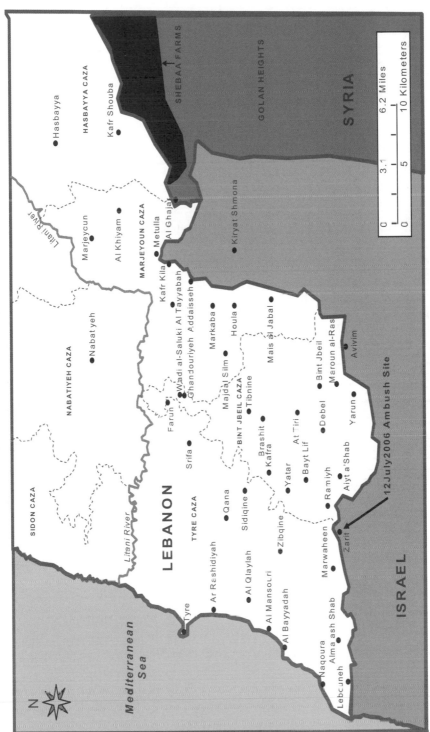

Map 2. The Ambush Site

35

It was not until 1003 that the battalion commander reported the specifics of the kidnapping to his brigade headquarters. It appears the brigade headquarters was roused into action 57 minutes later, and at 1100, a few armored vehicles crossed the border into Lebanon. As they moved rapidly toward a hill overlooking a possible Hezbollah escape route, a massive IED exploded beneath a Merkava 4 tank, sending heavy chunks of steel up to 150 yards away, instantly killing the crew of four. As rescue teams rushed forward to retrieve the bodies of the dead tank crew, two other IDF soldiers died during a vicious firefight with Hezbollah. At 1200, the IDF high command issued an order called the FOURTH DIMENSION, activating air strikes on 69 bridges in southern Lebanon. These strikes were meant to impede the kidnappers' escape.[9]

The IDF's response to the Hezbollah incursion and kidnapping on 12 July was a muddled, haphazard affair. From the failure to disseminate intelligence, to the lackadaisical approach of the soldiers on patrol, and the failure to rapidly pursue Hezbollah fighters, the operation revealed a stunning ineptitude on the part of the soldiers and leadership within the IDF. Sadly for Israel, the worst was yet to come.

Pulling the Levers

Around mid-afternoon on 12 July, Chief of the IDF General Staff Dan Halutz, Israeli Prime Minister Yossi Olmert, and Defense Minister Amir Peretz seized control of the situation and began planning their response to the kidnapping. Interestingly, both Olmert and Peretz had limited backgrounds in military affairs. In fact, Olmert had served as an IDF newspaper reporter, while Peretz fulfilled his military obligation as a maintenance officer.[10] The partial findings of the Winograd Report acknowledged that the Defense Minister "did not have knowledge or experience in military, political or governmental matters. He also did not have knowledge of the basic principles of using military force to achieve political goals." In formulating their response to the kidnapping, both Olmert and Peretz were forced to rely heavily on Halutz, a general who in every respect was unprepared for a full-scale ground war with Hezbollah.[11]

A few years prior to the outbreak of hostilities on 12 July, the IDF had drawn up two "well grounded" contingency plans to use against Hezbollah. The first was named ICE BREAKER (*SHOVERET HAKERACH*). This plan called for an air campaign against Hezbollah of 48 to 72 hours' duration. In tandem with ICE BREAKER was a ground invasion plan called MEY MAROM, designed to drive Hezbollah north of the Litani River. Author and IAF campaign planner Ron Tira recalled, "the idea was to simultaneously activate ICE BREAKER and call and deploy the

[IDF] reserves for MEY MAROM, and after 48–72 hours of air campaign to either exit the hostilities or activate MEY MAROM." Halutz rejected MEY MAROM, opting instead for a stand-alone air campaign.[12] Secretary of State Condoleeza Rice was allegedly told by the Israelis, "You did it in about 70 days [in Kosovo], but we need half of that—35 days."[13]

Halutz convinced Olmert and Peretz that Israel should strike back against Hezbollah and the Lebanese central government with a substantial air campaign. The plan was not designed to directly or fully crush Hezbollah's capabilities but to produce "effects" that would force Hezbollah out of southern Lebanon and cause them to disarm.[14] Halutz proposed an immense air strike against "symbolic" Lebanese targets and Hezbollah's military resources. The plan also called for targeted strikes against Hezbollah's military and political leadership. "His idea," Naveh stated, "was that . . . we hit all these targets [and] Hezbollah will collapse as a military organization. No one really believed that the Lebanese government was in position to really pressure Hezbollah. The idea was that Hezbollah would give up and then everybody would go home happy. Again, the idea was to change something in the equation; to change the conditions by forcing them to become political and abandon the military option."[15] Hezbollah, however, had prepared for an effects-based campaign, and the Lebanese government was too weak and incapable of challenging Hezbollah. There was simply no lever to pull that would cause Hezbollah to crumple.[16]

While some Israeli politicians and IDF officers were skeptical of Halutz's campaign plan, he failed to effectively address or present their doubts to Olmert and Peretz. The Winograd Report maintains Halutz did not reveal substantial deficiencies in the ground forces that may well thwart the success of their mission. Furthermore, he did not adequately address the fact that the military's own assessment indicated ground operations would most likely be warranted.[17]

The stage was now set to reveal to the world what one Israeli writer described as "a witches brew of high tech fantasies and basic unpreparedness."[18] On the night of 12 July, Israeli jets and artillery began limited attacks on infrastructure targets across Lebanon, Hezbollah's rockets, command and control centers, and its mouthpiece, al-Manar television. Just after midnight, an IAF squadron flying in the vicinity of Beirut attacked and destroyed 54 Hezbollah Zelzal rocket launchers. When Halutz received word of the mission's success, he informed Olmert by secure phone that "all the long-range rockets have been destroyed. We've won the war." Israel would soon learn that his declaration of mission accomplished could not have been further from the truth.[19]

Hezbollah Strikes Back

Nasrallah was completely taken aback by the massive Israeli bombardment. In fact, during an interview after the war, he admitted that "Hezbollah had made a terrible mistake in capturing two IDF soldiers and killing eight others on the morning of July 12, 2006."[20] On 14 July though, after IAF attacks on the Beirut airport and after the Israeli Navy blockaded all of Lebanon, Nasrallah delivered a taped message to the press. He announced to the Israelis, "You wanted an open war, and we are heading for an open war. We are ready for it." Augustus Richard Norton, a former military observer for the UN in southern Lebanon, wrote, "Nasrallah invited listeners to look to the sea, and with perfect theatrical timing an explosion on the horizon rocked the INS Hanit, an Israeli naval vessel that was hit by an Iranian-produced C-802 Noor guided missile."[21] The missile blasted a hole in the ship and killed four of its crew. Shockingly, the Eilat (Sa'ar 5)-class missile corvette had failed to activate its defense system against radar-guided antiship missiles. An Israeli rear admiral told a reporter from *Jane's* that "we were not aware that Hizbullah possessed this kind of missile."[22] As Norton pointed out, "This was an early hint that Hezbollah might have been better prepared than Israel presumed."[23]

Between 15 and 16 July, Israel continued to launch air and artillery strikes on Lebanon and Hezbollah. In turn, Hezbollah responded with a steady stream of rocket attacks on northern Israel. On 16 July, long-range Hezbollah rockets managed to fall on Haifa, Israel, killing eight Israelis, while the IAF killed at least 31 Lebanese in attacks across Lebanon.[24]

The next day, in a speech to the Knesset, Prime Minister Olmert announced Israel's war aims and detailed his own objectives that included the release of the two soldiers being held captive, as well as a cease-fire and withdrawal of Hezbollah forces from along the Lebanon border. Furthermore, Olmert called on the Lebanese army to be deployed in an effort to force Hezbollah out of the south. His most fervent aim, however, was that Hezbollah be abolished as a military power.[25]

The IAF's attacks on Hezbollah, however, proved ineffectual. Attempts to compromise its logistical sites and defensive positions in the opening three days of the war proved futile as did a targeted attack on Hezbollah's leadership in Beirut. A US official who closely monitored the war speculated that the IAF air strikes impacted only 7 percent of Hezbollah's military resources.[26]

As early as 14 July, Israeli intelligence suggested to high ranking military and political leaders that air power alone could not accomplish the mission. The intelligence "concluded that the heavy bombing campaign and small ground offensive [small IDF Special Forces incursions] then underway would show 'diminishing returns' within days. It stated that the plan would neither win the release of the two Israeli soldiers in Hezbollah's hands nor reduce the militia's rocket attacks on Israel to fewer than 100 a day."[27]

It soon became clear to some within the IDF that, if Israeli war aims were to be successfully prosecuted, the IDF would probably have to launch a major ground offensive into southern Lebanon. However, as Halutz and his senior commanders mulled over the situation, alarming reports began to trickle into headquarters from small IDF Special Forces units conducting probes into southern Lebanon. They reported, "Hezbollah units were fighting tenaciously to hold their positions on the first ridgeline overlooking Israel."[28]

Notes

1. Winograd Committee Interim Report, (Hebrew) 66-68; Ofer Shelah and Yaov Limor, Captives In Lebanon, (Hebrew) 21-63; Miskal, Yedioth Ahrononth and Chemed Books, 2007; "Eight IDF Soldiers Killed, 2 Kidnapped on Northern Frontier," *Jerusalem Post*, 12 July 2006.

2. Amir Oren, "Analysis: In Lebanon, Government Hamstrung Troubled Division," *Haaretz.com*, 15 October 2006, http://www.haaretz.com/hasen/spages/774974.html (accessed 1 July 2007).

3. *Haaretz.com* reported "that IDF investigations since the kidnapping showed that military intelligence ignored signs that Hezbollah was planning an attack." "Halutz appoints team to examine Hezbollah kidnapping of soldiers," Haaretz.com, 18 September 2006, http://www.haaretz.com/hasen/spages/764384.html (accessed 17 September 2007); Winograd Committee Interim Report, (Hebrew) 66-68; Ofer Shelah and Yaov Limor, Captives In Lebanon, (Hebrew) 21-63, Miskal, Yedioth Ahrononth and Chemed Books, 2007.

4. Winograd Committee Interim Report, (Hebrew) 66-68; Ofer Shelah and Yaov Limor, Captives In Lebanon, (Hebrew) 21-63, Miskal, Yedioth Ahrononth and Chemed Books, 2007.

5. It was recently revealed that the two IDF soldiers abducted by Hezbollah were probably mortally wounded in the incident. "Secret Report: Chances Captive Survived Are Slim." *Ynetnews.com*, http://www.ynetnews.com/articles/0,7340,L-3401556,00.html (accessed 17 September 2007).

6. Ibid.

7. Winograd Committee Interim Report, (Hebrew) 66-68; Ofer Shelah and Yaov Limor, Captives In Lebanon, (Hebrew) 21-63, Miskal, Yedioth Ahrononth and Chemed Books, 2007; "Hezbollah Kills 8 Soldiers, Kidnaps Two In Offensive On Northern Border," Haaretz.com, 13 July 2006, http://www.haaretz.com/hasen/pages/ShArt.jhtml?itemNo=737825 (accessed 18 September 2007).

8. Ibid.

9. Ibid; "IDF Spokesman: Hizbullah Attack On Northern Border and IDF Response," Israel Ministry of Foreign Affairs, 12 July 2006, http://www.mfa.gov.il/MFA/Terrorism-+Obstacle+to+Peace/Terrorism+from+Lebanon-+Hizbullah/Hizbullah+attack+on+northern+border+and+IDF+response+12-Jul-2006.htm (accessed 18 September 2007).

10. Ron Tira, e-mail interview by author, 19 September 2007.

11. Winograd Committee Interim Report, (Hebrew) 66-68; Ofer Shelah and Yaov Limor, Captives In Lebanon, (Hebrew) 21-63, Miskal, Yedioth Ahrononth and Chemed Books, 2007; The partial findings of the Winograd report stated that Halutz "failed in his duties as commander in chief of the army and as a critical part of the political-military leadership, and exhibited flaws in professionalism, responsibility and judgment." "The Winograd Report," Haaretz.com, 1 January 2007, http://www.haaretz.com/hasen/spages/854051.html (accessed 17 September 2007).

12. Ron Tira, e-mail interview by author, 20 June 2007.

13. Augustus Richard Norton, *Hezbollah: A Short History*, 139.

14. Uri Bar-Joseph, "Their Most Humiliating Hour," Haaretz.com, 27 April 2007, http://www.haaretz.com/hasen/spages/853115.html (accessed 19 September 2007).

15. Shimon Naveh, interview by author, 1 November 2007.

16. Ron Tira, e-mail interview by author, 16 August 2007.

17. "The Winograd Report: The main findings of the Winograd partial report on the Second Lebanon War," Haaretz.com, 1 January 2007, http://www.haaretz.com/hasen/spages/854051.html (accessed 18 September 2007).

18. "'The Revolution in Military Affairs' Shocks But Does Not Awe Israeli Commission," CDI Center For Defense Information, Straus Military Reform Project, 11 June 2007, http://www.cdi.org/friendlyversion/printversion.cfm?documentID=3977 (accessed 20 September 2007).

19. Uzi Mahnaimi, "Humbling of the Supertroops Shatters Israeli Army Morale," *TimesOnLine*, 27 August 2006, http://www.timesonline.co.uk/tol/news/world/article620874.ece (accessed 19 September 2007).

20. Nicholas Noe (ed), *Voice of Hezbollah: The Statements of Sayyed Hassan Nasrallah* (London: Verso, 2007), 378.

21. Augustus Richard Norton, *Hezbollah: A Short History*, (Princeton and Oxford: Princeton University Press, 2007), 136.

22. Alon Ben-David, *Jane's*, http://www.janes.com/defence/news/jdw/jdw060718_1_n.shtml (accessed 19 September 2007).

23. Norton, 136.

24. Jeremy M. Sharp, "Israel-Hamas-Hezbollah: The Current Conflict," CRS Report for Congress, Congressional Research Service, The Library of Congress, 21 July 2006, 34-37.

25. Norton, 139.

26. Alastair Crooke and Mark Perry, "How Hezbollah Defeated Israel, Part 1: Winning the Intelligence War," 5, http://www.atimes.com/atimes/Middle_East/HJ12Ak01.html (accessed 24 September 2007).

27. Scott Wilson, "Israeli War Plan Had No Exit Strategy," Washington Post.com, http://www.washingtonpost.com/wp-dyn/content/article/2006/10/20/AR2006102001688_pf.html (accessed 24 September 2007).

28. Alastair Crooke and Mark Perry, "How Hezbollah Defeated Israel, Part 2: Winning the Ground War," 2.

Chapter 4

The Ground War
17 July to 14 August

Evidently they had never heard that an Arab soldier is supposed to run away after a short engagement with the Israelis.

Unidentified Israeli Soldier

Anyone dumb enough to push a tank column through Wadi Saluki should not be an armored brigade commander but a cook.

Timur Goksel
Former Senior Advisor for UNIFIL

Maroun al-Ras and Bint Jbeil

In keeping with the new doctrine, Chief of the IDF General Staff Dan Halutz had no intention of implementing the ground invasion plan MEY MAROM and activating IDF reserve forces. Days into the war, he still felt the air campaign would succeed. However, Halutz was under pressure from army commanders to initiate a reserve callup in the event a full-scale ground invasion became necessary. Surprisingly, a compromise was reached between Halutz and his army generals that allowed the regular army to make limited battalion- and brigade-size raids into Lebanon. These initial raids were not designed to destroy Hezbollah or its rockets but to craft a "consciousness of victory" for the Israelis and a "cognitive perception of defeat" for Hezbollah. It became obvious to some within the IDF that this was utter nonsense. The air campaign could not destroy the Katyushas (falling on northern Israel at a rate of approximately 100 a day), and the proposed ground-based raids would certainly have little effect. As one distraught Israeli officer commented, "That didn't make sense at all. You either activate MEY MAROM [and] occupy the entire rocket launch area, or you don't—but there is absolutely no sense in raids. They were not going to stop the rockets, yet soldiers can get killed. It is risk without reward."[1]

On 17 July, the first large-scale Israeli ground foray began near Maroun al-Ras in an effort to establish a foothold in southern Lebanon.[2] One of the first units to come to blows with Hezbollah in Maroun al-Ras was the elite Maglan unit, part of what the IDF called a "special forces cluster."[3] "We didn't know what hit us," one Maglan soldier told a reporter. The Special Forces soldiers were stunned by the volume of gunfire and the doggedness of the Hezbollah fighters. Another Maglan reported, "We expected a tent and three Kalashnikovs—that was the intelligence we were given. Instead, we found a hydraulic steel door leading to a well-equipped network of tunnels." By the next morning, the Maglans were virtually surrounded. It was reported from northern headquarters that "the commander of the IDF's northern sector, Lieutenant-General Udi Adams, could barely believe that some of his best soldiers had been so swiftly trapped; neither could the chief of staff. 'What's wrong with the Maglans?' Halutz demanded to know. 'They are surrounded,' Adams replied quietly. 'I must send in more forces.'"[4]

From underground bunkers and tunnels, Hezbollah fighters in and around Maroun al-Ras fought back frantically. As the battle intensified, the IDF was forced to throw more forces into the fray. Soon, tanks from three Israeli brigades entered the fight, along with the Egoz unit from the Golani Brigade, an engineer battalion, and Battalion 101 of the Paratrooper Brigade. On 19 July, a Hezbollah antitank missile killed five Egoz soldiers as they sought shelter in a house.[5] At the same time, numerous IDF tanks were hit by Sagger antitank missiles, wounding many of the tank crewmen. "They're not fighting like we thought they would," one IDF soldier said. "They're fighting harder. They're good on their own ground." In fact, Hezbollah's tactical proficiency bewildered the IDF. Hezbollah was not simply hunkering down and defending terrain, but using its small arms, mortars, rockets, and antitank weapons to successfully maneuver against the IDF.[6]

Although some problems surrounding the IDF's performance in Maroun al-Ras remain murky, both officers and soldiers voiced major criticisms concerning tactics and casualties. Early in the fight, reports circulated that growing concern over casualties caused IDF commanders to become overly cautious. Reports also confirmed a lack of combined arms expertise and a deficiency in basic tactical skills.[7] Years of COIN operations against the Palestinians had greatly eroded the IDF's conventional warfighting proficiency. An IDF general pointed out, "It's one thing to give the troops maps, target list, etc. It's another thing to be trained for the mission—they weren't trained. . . ."[8]

Taken aback by the ineffective air campaign and surprised by Hezbollah's stubborn resistance in Maroun al-Ras, Olmert and Halutz called up Israeli reserve forces on 21 July. One source concluded that "the decision to call the reserves took key senior reserve officers, usually the first to be notified of a pending call-up, by surprise. The reserve callup was handled chaotically—with the reserve 'tail' of logistical support lagging some 24–48 hours behind the deployment of reserve forces."[9] Contrary to the opinion of some, the callup was not designed to assist the regular army in a massive ground invasion of southern Lebanon. Although it would allow Israel to amass forces along the border, Hulutz's ground plan would remain unchanged. There would be no determined effort to drive Hezbollah back across the Litani or destroy its rockets with a large-scale ground assault. A general on Hulutz's staff told a reporter on 22 July that "The goal is not necessarily to eliminate every Hezbollah rocket. What we must do is disrupt the military logic of Hezbollah. I would say that this is still not a matter of days away." Many ground commanders were stunned by the remark and questioned the true aims of the war.[10]

On the same day the IDF reserve forces were called to duty, Israel was forced to request an emergency resupply of precision-guided missiles from the United States. In 10 days, the IAF had used up most of its high-tech munitions, and yet, this huge expenditure of weaponry did little to change Hezbollah's "military logic" or its fighting capability. Mossad was already gathering information to leak to the press on 28 July, indicating "Hezbollah had not suffered a significant degradation in its military capabilities, and that the organization might be able to carry on the conflict for several months."[11]

Undeterred by the failure of the air campaign and stiff Hezbollah resistance, Halutz and his staff continued efforts to secure a "consciousness of victory" and to deliver to Hezbollah a "cognitive perception of defeat." By 24 July, elements of the Golani Brigade and the 7th Armor Brigade had established overwatch positions around Bint Jbeil, a large town north of Maroun al-Ras. On 25 July, the 35th Paratrooper Brigade began moving northwest of the town in an attempt to establish a blocking position. The same day, the Division 91 Commander, Brigadier General Gal Hirsch, a man considered both "brilliant" and "arrogant," announced to the press that his forces were in control of Bint Jbeil.[12] This, however, was not the case. As Hezbollah rockets continued to rain down on Israel and kill Israeli citizens, Halutz ordered the commander of IDF northern forces, Lieutenant-General Udi Adam, to attack the town. Hezbollah Secretary-General Nasrallah had delivered his well-known victory speech in Bint Jbeil after the 2000 Israeli withdrawal from Lebanon. Halutz asserted that capturing the town would prove symbolic and "create a spectacle of victory." This "spectacle of victory" was undoubtedly designed to effect the cognitive perception of Hezbollah. In the end, however, the battle for Bint Jbeil would have a great deal more effect on the Israeli public's perception of the IDF's professionalism and judgment.[13]

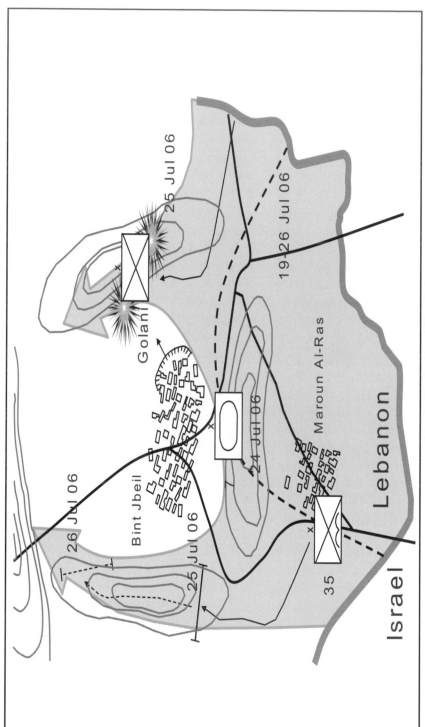

Map 3. The Battle of Bint Jbeil

Halutz ordered Adams to "conquer Bint Jbeil" with just one battalion. Adam was infuriated and quickly reminded his commander that "the casbah [old quarter] of Bint Jbail alone contained more than 5,000 houses. And you want me to send in one battalion?" Adam's protests were to no avail and on 26 July, after an intense artillery bombardment of the town, the 51st Battalion of the Golani Brigade maneuvered into Bint Jbeil from the east.[14] In the midst of the artillery barrage, additional Hezbollah fighters took up positions in the town.[15] This would not be the last time Hezbollah's intelligence apparatus accurately predicted an impending IDF offensive.[16]

At 0530, Companies A and C of the 51st Battalion ran headlong into a withering array of Hezbollah small arms, machine guns, rocket-propelled grenades (RPGs), antitank missiles, mortars, and short-range rockets.[17] "An ambush from hell" is how one Israeli soldier described the first contact. "The Hezbollah men were in upper stories of buildings," another soldier remembered "and had a commanding view of the IDF force. In the initial firing, 30 members of C Company, one third of its total strength, were hit, as was the battalion's Deputy Commander, Major Roi Klein." Company A also sustained five casualties. As the fighting intensified, Hezbollah squads maneuvered onto their flanks and continued to deliver a multitude of direct and indirect fires. Companies A and C continued to resist the violent attacks, as other companies from the 51st Battalion rushed forward to assist with the evacuation of dead and wounded.[18]

An eyewitness reported on the chaotic events at the Golani Brigade's headquarters, noting "emotions ran high as word came in of the fierce gun-battle and heavy casualties. Soldiers ran back and forth with maps and officers screamed into encrypted cellular phones coordinating the evacuation of the wounded. At one point Brig. Gen. Gal Hirsh . . . stepped out of the command center to update . . . Halutz. 'We can't land the helicopters,' he said, 'The fighting is too intense.'"[19] It would take all night to evacuate the wounded and the dead. In all, 9 soldiers died and 27 were wounded.[20] Ultimately, Hezbollah fighters continued to occupy Bint Jbeil. Even by the close of the war, the town was never entirely secured by the IDF.

While Hezbollah's television station al-Manar (which the IAF failed to knock off the air) continued to broadcast glowing reports of its successful battle with the IDF, Israeli state-owned television denounced the IDF and what it called "idiotic military maneuvers." Israeli print media also harassed the IDF with "three front page columns" asking "Was there a proper decision process? No Goals attained," and "Has the army failed?"[21] To make matters worse, international opinion (which early on had denounced Hezbollah for the kidnapping) turned against Israel as the IAF continued to attack Lebanon's infrastructure and inadvertently kill Lebanese civilians.[22] Like the air and ground campaign, the IDF's media campaign was floundering. Contrary to Halutz's game plan, the media was projecting "a cognitive perception of defeat" onto the IDF and the Israeli public.

By the last days of July, however, Halutz remained convinced that his method was still viable. Choosing not to follow the counsel of senior staff and initiate a massive ground offensive, Halutz implemented a more conservative "enter and pull out" strategy. This was met with some skepticism. Major General Ido Nehushtan advised Halutz on 26 July:

> . . . that without a major ground campaign, the IDF could not stop the Katyusha rockets. You must bring this before the government. You need to tell them straight that without a major ground operation, we cannot remove the Katyusha threat. If the government does not approve it [a large pre-planned ground offensive], we should tell them that they must stop the campaign now. The fact is that the war between the IDF and Hezbollah we can describe as a draw. . . . We should tell the political echelon that we cannot limit [the Katyusha attacks] any more than we are now doing, except if we take over [the ground] up to the Litani [River].[23]

Despite these observations, by 1 August, the IDF was still conducting only small battalion- and brigade-size raids into southern Lebanon. On that date, the IDF reported that, "during extensive initiated activities intended to hurt Hezbollah['s] organization [al] infrastructures, infantry corps, engineering, and armor forces took positions last night (Tuesday 01/08/06) in the area of the villages of Mis El Jabel, Jabel, Mahbib, and Belidah. Simultaneously, the forces strengthened their hold on the villages of A-Teiba, El-Adisa, and Rav A-Tietin, west of Metula, and the villages Ayta A-Sha'ab, Maorun A-Ras, and Bint-Jbeil."[24] In the fighting around Ayta A-Shab, 2 IDF soldiers were killed and 25 wounded.[25]

"In one day in 1982," Timur Goksel, a former senior advisor for UNIFIL, concluded, "they [the IDF] reached Beirut; here, in six or seven days, they couldn't go more than a few miles."[26] Irritated by the lack of success, Halutz replaced northern sector Commander Lieutenant-General Udi Adams with his own "personal representative," Major General Moshe Kaplinsky. According to some sources, Kaplinsky was "to manage the war."[27]

The Reserves

The true magnitude of the ground forces' fragility became increasingly evident as IDF reserve units began to assemble near the border. One highly credible source concluded, "Hezbollah commanders found that Israeli troops were poorly organized and disciplined. . . . IDF commanders were also disturbed by the performance of their troops, noting a signal lack of discipline even among its best-trained soldiers. The reserves were worse, and IDF commanders hesitated to put them into battle."[28]

A reserve soldier in a combat infantry brigade told a reporter:

> In the past six years I've only had a week's training. Soon after we arrived, we received an order to seize a nearby Shi'ite village. We knew that we were not properly trained for the mission. We told our commanders we could control the village with firepower and there was no need to take it and be killed for nothing. Luckily we were able to convince our commander. . . . For the last six years we were engaged in stupid policing missions in the West Bank. . . . Checkpoints, hunting stone-throwing Palestinian children, that kind of stuff. The result was that we were not ready to confront real fighters like Hezbollah.

A reserve engineering officer who was ordered to clear a road running into Bint Jbeil refused, his men complaining that "10 soldiers had already died there." The brigade commander had the entire platoon arrested and carted off to jail.[29]

IDF soldiers in the reserve paratrooper division were continually perplexed by their orders. "From time to time they got orders to seek out Hizbollah on the ground, but every time the orders were cancelled at the last minute," a journalist reported. When they asked their division commander for an explanation after the war, "he said they didn't want us to get killed or kidnapped by Hizbollah, or by all the friendly fire that was going on." It was later revealed "that in many cases, the reluctance to send Israeli troops into battle against Hizbullah grew out of the realization by commanding officers that the soldiers would have been going on suicide missions."

One paratrooper platoon had only two light antitank weapons (LAWs) for 30 men. "I've never fired a LAW in my life," a soldier in the platoon stated. "When Hizbullah is firing antitank missiles at us, how do I respond?" Many of the reserve soldiers who arrived at their bases to receive their military equipment found basic items missing from their kitbags. There was also a lack of bulletproof vests, medical vests, radios, ammunition, thermal night-vision devices, as well as food and water.[30]

Some IDF reserve units conducting cross-border attacks against Hezbollah often found themselves without basic sustenance as their supply trucks were not allowed to go forward for fear of Hezbollah's antitank missiles. In the Alexandroni Brigade, one of the unit's missions was delayed because of the lack of food and water. A reservist in the brigade noted, "We went as long as two-and-a-half days with daily rations of a can of tuna, a can of corn and a couple of pieces of bread—to share between four soldiers. So we got slowed up because 25 soldiers collapsed from dehydration and had to be evacuated."[31]

Incredibly, even the reserve division commanders lacked training and appeared to be both tactically and technically deficient. Brigadier General Erez Zuckerman, who commanded the reserve armored division, had spent most of his career as a marine commando and had never received training in the use of tanks or mechanized forces. Brigadier General Eyal Eizenberg, the commander of the reserve paratrooper division, was singled out for "harsh criticism" for his apparent lack of tactical proficiency.[32] There can be little doubt that the IDF reserve forces lacked leadership, training, and equipment. This was a serious detriment as these citizen soldiers comprised nearly 80 percent of the IDF's ground forces.[33]

Battle of Awareness and the Drive to the Litani

By 5 August, the IDF had approximately 10,000 soldiers in southern Lebanon. In three weeks of war, the ground forces managed to penetrate no farther than four miles. Remarkably, the border zone remained unsecured, as were the towns of Maroun al Ras and Bint Jbeil.[34] Yet, the entire Hezbollah force south of the Litani consisted of only 3,000 fighters. Unlike the IDF, Hezbollah did not call on its sizable reserve forces and chose to fight the entire war south of the Litani with its original force of 3,000 men.[35] For Israel and the IDF, there was still no "spectacle of victory" or any sign of Hezbollah's impending defeat.

"They are experts at deception," a soldier pointed out after weeks of battling Hezbollah. "Everyone will think they won no matter what. That's how you win when there's a few thousand of you and 50,000 of us. The more of them we kill, the more of them who are generated. Unfortunately, this is a lost war." As Hezbollah rockets continued to kill Israeli civilians, IDF ground forces continued to battle their elusive foe. Many of the IDF soldiers were amazed by Hezbollah's elaborate bunker and tunnel system. One infantryman reported finding a bunker near Maroun al-Ras "that was more than 25 feet deep and contained a network of tunnels linking several large storage rooms and multiple entrances and exits. He said it was equipped with a camera at the entrance, linked to a monitor below to help Hezbollah fighters ambush Israeli soldiers."[36]

While the IDF had some tactical successes, one senior Israeli intelligence officer remarked that Hezbollah fighters had "gone to school" on IDF ground forces and described the foe as "an infantry brigade with modern weapons." By 8 August, 61 Israeli soldiers had been killed, while the IDF reported 450 Hezbollah fighters killed. This last figure was highly exaggerated, as it appears likely that only 184 Hezbollah fighters were killed in ground fighting in southern Lebanon during the entire war.[37]

While many within the IDF and the Israeli public remained perplexed over Halutz's effects-based ground campaign of "raids" and "enter and pull out missions," retired Israeli politicians and seasoned IDF officers became increasingly alarmed. One report stated:

> As the fighting dragged on, some veteran officers lost patience with what they saw as the inexperience of the chief of staff and defence minister. 'What are you doing in Lebanon, for God's sake?' the former defence minister, General Shaul Mofaz, asked Olmert. 'Why did you go into Bint Jbeil? It was a trap set by Hezbollah.' Mofaz proposed an old-fashioned IDF assault plan to launch a blitzkrieg against Hezbollah, reach the strategically important Litani River in 48 hours and then demolish Hezbollah in six days. Olmert liked the idea but Peretz did not appreciate his predecessor's intervention and rejected it. Olmert appeared to lose confidence and began to issue conflicting orders. 'Our mission changed twice, three times every day,' complained one soldier. Many Israelis have been left furious that the legendary deterrent power of their army has been shattered.[38]

On 11 August, the UN Security Council unanimously approved Resolution 1701, which was designed to implement a cease-fire and end the war as soon as possible. A UN press release declared "the utmost concern at the spiraling deadly violence and destruction in Lebanon" and called "for a full cessation of hostilities in the month-long war between Israel and Hizbollah, mapping out a formula for the phased withdrawal of the Israel Defence Forces from southern Lebanon, while up to 15,000 United Nations peacekeepers help Lebanese troops take control of the area."[39]

Knowing full well that the war would be over in days and the old border reestablished, Olmert and Peretz made the decision to expand the war effort by ordering their divisions north to the Litani. It was perhaps one of the most bizarre episodes of the war. While the reasoning for the offensive maneuver remains clouded, the move was clearly not designed to annihilate Hezbollah. Ron Tira was certain that "at no point was an order given to systemically and comprehensively deal with the rockets or Hezbollah."[40] It would appear that the IDF was still following Halutz's "raid" strategy, albeit this time with divisions instead of battalions and brigades.[41] Senior IDF officers would later state that the operation was designed as a "Battle of Awareness against Hizbollah." Others thought the operation was designed as "a kind of show designed to demonstrate to Hizbollah who is the Boss."[42]

On 11 August, the airborne reserve division under Eyal Eizenberg began moving north toward Dibel and Qana. Two Hezbollah antitank missiles hit a dwelling packed with 50 paratroopers after two of Eizenberg's companies were ordered to take up positions in houses in Dibel during daylight hours. The resulting explosion killed 9 and wounded 31 soldiers from the demolition company. By the time the official cease-fire went into effect on 14 August, Eizenberg's paratrooper division had managed to advance about one mile north of Dibel.[43] Along the coastal road, west of Eizenberg, unidentified IDF mechanized units managed to advance about one mile north of Mansuri by the time the war ended on 14 August.

Meanwhile, Brigadier General Gal Hirsch's Division 91 began its trek toward the Mediterranean coast, moving west from north of Bint Jbeil, where pockets of Hezbollah fighters still remained. The action proved chaotic, similar to attacks on Maroun al-Ras and Bint Jbeil. After the war, an official government investigation revealed a stunning lack of professionalism and competence in Division 91. The investigation concluded that commanders within the division "did not fully understand their orders" and "were not present with their troops during important battles and even failed to fulfill basic missions." The investigation also found fault "in the way tactical orders were composed, sometimes without a time element. Since the orders were not clear, they were changed, in some cases, on an hourly basis. Brigade commanders did not properly understand their missions. . . . They didn't know what their goals were and how long they had to fulfill their missions." Remarkably, according to the report, "an entire battalion sat in the same location for several days without moving and when the commander finally received orders to push deeper into enemy territory he was confused and failed to fulfill the mission."[44]

Some of the problems within Division 91 were caused by Hirsch's operation orders. Instead of using the standard terms and format in writing

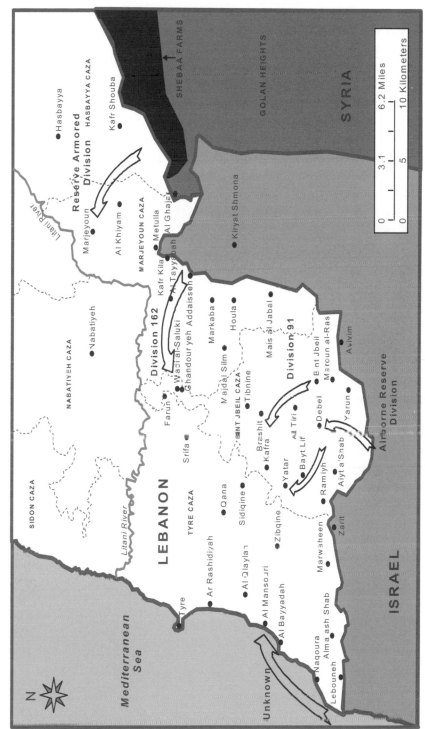

Map 4. Drive to the Litani

53

his orders, Hirsch used the terminology and methodology from Halutz's new doctrine. Israeli Air Force campaign planner Ron Tira, who reviewed the orders after the war, wrote that "when Division 91 gave its battle orders to its brigades, the orders were such that they were impossible to understand."[45] Not surprisingly, Division 91's drive to the Mediterranean fell far short of the mark by war's end.

Northeast of Division 91, Brigadier General Guy Tzur's Division 162 began its drive west from Metulla toward Qantara and Ghandouriyeh. Situated on the high ground overlooking the Litani, with east-west and north-south roads running through it, Tzur's Division saw Ghandouriyeh as a key piece of terrain. For over a week, Tsur planned to capture the town, but each time his division initiated the orders, higher headquarters abruptly canceled them.

In an effort to provide cover for the tanks and clear the high ground above Wadi al-Saluki, Division 162 air assaulted in elements of the Nahal Brigade. The soldiers apparently landed unopposed on the outskirts of Farun and Ghandouriyeh. It is likely that the soldiers of the Nahal Brigade occupied several buildings in the two Lebanese towns and did little in the way of clearing the high ground above the Wadi. On 12 August, however, they informed their commander that the area was secure.[46]

With the high ground presumably secure, 24 tanks of Brigade 401 began crossing the Wadi al-Saluki. Soon after moving forward, the two lead tanks in the column found their route blocked by a collapsed building. As the tanks searched for another crossing point, a large IED or mine exploded behind them, collapsing the road. At precisely the same moment, a Hezbollah Kornet laser-guided antitank missile slammed into a company commander's Merkava, killing him and the entire crew. Within seconds, swarms of antitank missiles assailed the tank column. Amazingly, the IDF reported that every single tank crew in the Wadi failed to use the smoke screen system on their tanks to help protect them from the deadly missiles.[47] One of the ambushed tank crewmen recalled, "When the first tank was hit, we knew that the nightmare had begun. You should understand that the first missile which hits is not the really dangerous missile. The ones which come afterward are the dangerous ones—and there always follow four or five after the first. . . . It was hellfire, and have no idea when it will get you. You just pray that it will end at last, that the volley will end and that you will hear on the radio that everybody is OK. But, unfortunately, that is not what we heard when the shooting ended, no sir!"[48]

Pinned down by Hezbollah antitank missiles, direct-fire weapons, and mortars, the infantry soldiers of the Nahal Brigade were hard pressed to lend support to the tank column.[49] "We thought that we were entering the Saluki after the area had been cleaned up, but then the terrorists came out of the houses and hiding places and started shooting at us as if we [were] in a shooting range," another tank crewman remembered.[50] Incredibly, there was no coordination whatsoever between the infantry and the tanks, and frantic calls from the trapped tank command for artillery and air support were denied by Northern Command due to concerns over fratricide.[51]

By the time the ambush ended, 11 of the 24 Merkava 4 tanks in Wadi al-Saluki had been hit by antitank missiles.[52] Eight tank crewmen and four infantrymen were killed. Although the exact number of wounded is not yet established, both the battalion commander and his deputy in the tank column suffered injuries.[53] It would appear that, by the time the cease-fire went into effect, Division 162 had advanced no farther than Ghandouriyeh. An officer from Division 162 stated, "There were many professional mistakes made in the use of the tanks. The soldiers were not trained properly for this battle and the division lacked experience in using tanks and infantry units operating together and in this type of terrain."[54] Undoubtedly, the actions of Division 162 at Wadi al-Saluki underscore the dismal state of the IDF's ground forces, particularity in conducting conventional maneuver operations.

To the north of Tzur's Division 162, Brigadier General Erez Zuckerman's reserve armored division was also having difficulty implementing the so-called "Battle of Awareness." While the operations of the reserve armored division remains sketchy, there appears to have been major problems within the command. Zuckerman was "castigated" by an official IDF investigative team after the war for the poor performance of his tank units. The report also stated that "his lack of training led to many failures."[55] Zuckerman would later relinquish his command, telling his superiors that "I have failed and I resign. . . . Toward the end of the war I felt that I had failed in my duty and decided to take personal responsibility. . . . I told this to my commanders and subordinates every chance I got."[56] According to an Israeli source, out of 11 IDF brigade commanders, only one ever crossed the border into Lebanon by wars' end.[57]

On 13 August, one day before the cease-fire, the IDF conducted air assaults and airborne drops south of the Litani. These air assaults and airborne drops were intended to expand Israeli control to the Litani. This decision could easily have had calamitous results if not for the implementation of the cease-fire. According to one source, most of the IDF soldiers were "immediately surrounded" once they hit the ground. Although many regarded the decision as purely political, one retired IDF officer went so far as to assert that Olmert was "using the military for public relations purposes."[58]

Halutz monitored these last missions from inside his bunker in Tel Aviv. When he received word that one of the IDF's Sikorsky CH-53 helicopters had been shot down by Hezbollah, killing the entire crew, the chief of staff purportedly exclaimed that he "felt defeated, both personally and professionally." Hezbollah, in a final act of defiance, fired 250 rockets into Israel in the closing hours before the cease-fire.[59]

Notes

1. Ron Tira, e-mail interview by author, 20, 21 June 2007.

2. Andrew Exum, "Hizballah at War: A Military Assessment," The Washington Institute for Near East Policy, Policy Focus No. 63, December 2006, 9.

3. Alex Fishman, "The Changing Face of the IDF: The Security Agenda and the Ballot Box," *Strategic Assessment*, Jaffee Center for Strategic Studies, Vol. 8, No. 4 (February 2006), 6, http://www.tau.ac.il/jcss/sa/v8n4p3Fishman. html (accessed 25 September 2007).

4. Uzi Mahnaimi, *The Sunday Times*, 27 August 2006, http://www. timesonline.co.uk/tol/news/world/article620874.ece (accessed 24 September 2007).

5. Ibid.

6. Exum, 10.

7. *Jerusalem Post*, 24 July 2006.

8. Exum, 10.

9. Alastair Crooke and Mark Perry, "How Hezbollah Defeated Israel, Part 2: Winning The Ground War." http://www.atimes.com/atimes/Middle_East/ IIJ13Ak01.html (accessed 1 September 2007), 2.

10. Ibid.

11. Ibid.

12. Amos Harel, "Caught Between The Pride Of Combat And The Public's Criticism," Haaretz.com, 4 November 2006, http://www.haaretz.com/hasen/ spages/783040.html (accessed 4 October 2007).

13. Uri Bar-Joseph, "Their Most Humiliating Hour," Haaretz.com, 27 April 2007, http://www.haaretz.com/hasen/spages/853115.html (accessed 23 September 2007).

14. Ibid, 3-4.

15. "Bint Jbeil: Hezbollah Heartland," BBC News, http://news.bbc.co.uk/2/ hi/middle_east/5221086.stm (accessed 19 September 2007).

16. Alastair Crooke and Mark Perry, "How Hezbollah Defeated Israel, Part 1," 8.

17. Mitchell Prothero, "The Day Israel Realized That This Was A Real War," *Guardian Unlimited*, 30 July 2006, http://observer.guardian.co.uk/world/ story/0,,1833349,00.html (accessed 4 October 2007); "9 IDF Troops Killed In Day Of Fighting," *Ynetnews.com*, http://www.ynetnews.com/articles/0,7340,L-3281856,00.html (accessed 4 October 2007).

18. Anshel Pfeffer, "It was all so very fast-the shooting, the shouting," *Jerusalem Post Online Edition*, 28 July 2007, http://www.jpost.com/servlet/Satel lite?cid=1153292016359&pagename=JPost%2FJPArticle%2FPrinter (accessed 4 October 2007).

19. Yaakov Katz, "Names Of Nine Soldiers Killed In Lebanon Released," *Jerusalem Post Online Edition,* http://info.jpost.com/C002/Supplements/ CasualtiesOfWar/2006_07_26.html (accessed 4 October 2007).

20. Anshel Pfeffer, "It was all so very fast-the shooting, the shouting," *Jerusalem Post Online Edition*, 28 July 2007; "Deadly Battles In Bint Jbeil: Fallen Soldiers' Stories," *Ynetnews.com*, http://www.ynetnews.com/articles/0,7340,L-3282017,00.html (accessed 4 October 2007).

21. Uzi Mahnaimi, "Humbling Of The Supertroops Shatters Israeli Army Morale," 4; Aron Heller, "Lebanon Offensive Criticized In Israel," *Washingtonpost.com*, 26 July 2006, http://www.washingtonpost.com/wp-dyn/content/article/2006/07/26/AR2006072601156_pf.html (accessed 1 October 2007).

22. Augustus Richard Norton, *Hezbollah: A Short History* (Princeton and Oxford: Princeton University Press, 2007), 136–140.

23. "IDF Shake-Up Over Hezbollah War," The Jewish Institute for National Security Affairs, *JINSA Online*, 23 March 2007, http://www.jinsa.org/articles/articles.html/function/view/categoryid/154/documentid/3736/history/3,2360,654,154,3736 (accessed 5 October 2007), 6.

24. "IDF Forces Continue Extensive Ground Operations in Southwest Lebanon," Israel Defense Forces: The Official Website, 02/08/2006, http://1.idf.il/DOVER/site/mainpage.asp?sl=EN&id=7&docid=55441&Pos=101&last (accessed 1 September 2007).

25. Israel Defense Forces: The Official Website, 55429&Pos=103&last (accessed 2 September 2007).

26. Captain Daniel Helmer, "Not Quite Counterinsurgency: A Cautionary Tale for US Forces Based on Israel's Operation Change of Direction," *Armor* Vol. CXVI, No. 1 (January–February 2007): 8.

27. David Makovsky and Jeffrey White, "Lessons And Implications Of The Israel-Hezbollah War: A Preliminary Assessment," The Washington Institute for Near East Policy, Policy Focus No. 60, October 2006, 50.

28. Alastair Crooke and Mark Perry, "How Hezbollah Defeated Israel, Part 2: Winning The Ground War," 5.

29. Uzi Mahnaimi, "Humbling Of The Supertroops Shatters Israeli Army Morale," *TimesOnline, The Sunday Times*, 4.

30. Larry Derfner, "Lambs To The Slaughter?" *Jerusalem Post Online Edition*, 24 August 2006, http://www.jpost.com/servlet/Satellite?cid=1154525936658&pagename=JPost/JPArticle/ShowFull (accessed 15 October 2007), 1-4.

31. Ibid.

32. Josh Brannon, "Halutz Slammed For Promoting Lebanon War Generals," *Jerusalem Post Online Edition*, 30 October 2007, http://www.jpost.com/servlet/Satellite?pagename=JPost%2FJPArticle%2FShowFull&cid=1161811237367 (accessed 5 October 2007); Amos Harel, "Seven Months On, The IDF Implementing Lessons Of The Lebanon War," www.haaretz.com, http://www.haaretz.com/hasen/spages/822989.html (accessed 7 October 2007); Yossi Yehoshua, "Lebanon War Commander Resigns," *Ynetnews.com*, http://www.ynetnews.com/articles/0,7340,L-3407286,00.html (accessed 7 October 2007).

33. Larry Derfner, "Lambs To The Slaughter," 3.

34. Captain Daniel Helmer, "Not Quite Counterinsurgency: A Cautionary

Tale for US Forces Based on Israel's Operation Change of Direction," 8.

35. Greg Myre, "Risks Escalate As Israel Fights A Ground War," *The New York Times*, 5 August 2006, http://www.nytimes.com/2006/08/05/world/middleeast/05zone.html (accessed 1 October 2007); Crooke and Perry, "How Hezbollah Defeated Israel, Part 2," 5.

36. Jonathan Finer, "Israeli Soldiers Find A Tenacious Foe In Hezbollah," *WashingtonPost.com*, 8 August 2006, http://www.washingtonpost.com/wp-dyn/content/article/2006/08/07/AR2006080701453.html (accessed 9 October 2007), 1-4.

37. Crooke and Perry, "How Hezbollah Defeated Israel, Part 2," 10.

38. Uzi Mahnaimi, "Humbling Of The Supertroops Shatters Israeli Army Morale," 5.

39. "Security Council Calls For End To Hostilities Between Hizbollah, Israel," United Nations Security Council SC/8808, 11 August 2006, http://www.un.org/News/Press/docs/2006/sc8808.doc.htm (accessed 10 October 2007).

40. Ron Tira, e-mail interview by author, 11 July 2007.

41. Ibid.

42. Nava Tzuriel and Eitan Glickman, "The Canyon Of Death," trans. by Adam Keller, *Yediot Aharonot*, 16 August 2006, 1. http://www.kibush.co.il/show_file.asp?num=15859 (accessed 1 October 2007).

43. Josh Brannon, "Halutz Slammed For Promoting Lebanon War Generals," *Jerusalem Post Online Edition*, 30 October 2007, http://www.jpost.com/servlet/Satellite?pagename=JPost%2FJPArticle%2FShowFull&cid=1161811237367 (accessed 5 October 2007); Amos Harel, "Seven Months On, The IDF Implementing Lessons Of The Lebanon War," www.haaretz.com, http://www.haaretz.com/hasen/spages/822989.html (accessed 7 October 2007); Yossi Ychoshua, "Lebanon War Commander Resigns," Ynetnews.com, http://www.ynetnews.com/articles/0,7340,L-3407286,00.html (accessed 7 October 2007).

44. Yaakov Katz, "Commanders Failed To Fulfill Missions," *Jerusalem Post Online Edition*, 15 October 2006, http://www.jpost.com/servlet/Satellite?cid=1159193446682&pagename=JPost%2FJPArticle%2FShowFull (accessed 11 October 2007).

45. Ron Tira, e-mail interview by author, 19 June 2007.

46. Captain Daniel Helmer, "Not Quite Counterinsurgency: A Cautionary Tale for US Forces Based on Israel's Operation Change of Direction," *Armor* Vol. CXVI, No. 1 (January February 2007), 7-11.

47. Yaakov Katz, "Post-battle Probe Finds Merkava Tank Misused In Lebanon," *Jerusalem Post Online Edition*, 3 September 2006, http://www.jpost.com/servlet/Satellite?cid=1154525995589&pagename=JPost%2FJPArticle%2FPrinter (accessed 5 October 2007).

48. Nava Tzuriel and Eitan Glickman, "The Canyon Of Death," *Yediot Aharonot*, 16 August 2006, 2.

49. Helmer, "Not Quite Counterinsurgency," 10.

50. "The Canyon Of Death," 2.

51. Yaakov Katz, "Wadi Saluki Battle Microcosm Of War's Mistakes,"

Jerusalem Post Online Edition, 29 August 2006, http://www.jpost.com/servlet/
Satellite?cid=1154525969154&pagename=JPost%2FJPArticle%2FShowFull
(accessed 15 September 2007), 1-2.

52. Katz, "Wadi Saluki Battle," 2.

53. Helmer, "Not Quite Counterinsurgency," 9-10; Nava Tzuriel and Eitan
Glickman "The Canyon Of Death," 3.

54. Katz, "Wadi Saluki Battle," 2.

55. Amos Harel, "Seven Months On, The IDF Implementing Lessons Of
Lebanon War," *Haaretz.com*, http://www.haaretz.com/hasen/spages/822989.html
(accessed 10 October 2007).

56. "Lebanon War Commander Resigns," *Ynetnews.com*, http://www.
ynetnews.com/articles/0,7340,L-3407286,00.html (accessed 1 October 2007).

57. Yaakov Katz, "Commanders Failed To Fulfill Missions," *Jerusalem Post
Online Edition*, 15 October 2006, http://www.jpost.com/servlet/Satellite?cid=115
9193446682&pagename=JPost%2FJPArticle%2FShowFull (accessed 12 October
2007).

58. Crooke and Perry, "How Hezbollah Defeated Israel, Part 2," 9.

59. Uzi Mahnaimi, "Humbling Of The Supertroops Shatters Israeli Army
Morale," 5; Andrew Exum, "Hizballah at War: A Military Assessment," 12.

Conclusions

> The IDF was not ready for this war.
>
> The Winograd Report

By the time the UN crease-fire went into effect on 14 August, Hezbollah had launched 3,790 rockets in Israeli territory. A total of 901 of these rockets hit Israeli towns and cities, killing 42 civilians and wounding 4,262. An additional 2,773 Israeli civilians were treated for "shock and anxiety."[1] The war was a wakeup call for Israel. The Effects-Based Operations (EBO) and Systemic Operational Design (SOD)-inspired doctrine that vigorously embraced air power at the expense of a classic ground maneuver campaign was certainly a major factor in the IDF's disappointing performance. As IAF campaign planner Ron Tira noted:

> Israel failed on the strategic, operational, and tactical levels. Israel did not succeed in generating decapitation, paralysis, blindness, or any other effect that substantially harms the will or functioning of the organization's command and control echelon. Nor did it succeed in suppressing the operational effectiveness of Hizbollah's combat groups and light surface-to-surface rocket formations. At the end of the day, Israel did not upset the equilibrium of Hizbollah's system and did not create a sense of helplessness and distress, nor did it push the organization towards cognitive-strategic collapse and a drive to end the war immediately on Israel's terms.[2]

As enemy rockets rained down on northern Israel, the IDF attempted to orchestrate the strategic cognitive collapse of Hezbollah through the use of air power and precision firepower-based operations. When this failed, the IDF sought to produce the same effects by using its ground forces to conduct limited raids and probes into southern Lebanon. These restrained initiatives designed to create a cognitive perception of defeat also failed to produce the effects necessary to incapacitate Hezbollah. The presence of several IDF mechanized divisions north of the Litani in the first 72 hours of the war, combined with a violent, systematic clearing of Hezbollah's bunkers and tunnels, might have brought about the cognitive collapse Halutz so desperately sought. Unfortunately, the new IDF doctrine failed to incorporate a large land maneuver component into its effects-based approach.

According to Ron Tira, one of the major problems within the IDF was "the over-zealous embrace of the American effects-based operations

(EBO) idea. EBO's aim is to paralyze the enemy's operational ability, in contrast to destroying its military force. This is achieved by striking the headquarters, lines of communication, and other critical junctions in the military structure. EBO [was] employed in their most distinct form in the Shock and Awe campaign that opened the 2003 Iraq War. However, the Americans used EBO to prepare the way for their ground maneuvers, and not as an alternative to them."[3]

Unfortunately for Israel, the new commander of the IDF warmly embraced this new philosophy. The ascension of Lieutenant-General Dan Halutz to the position of Chief of the IDF General Staff in June 2005 marked the first time in the history of Israel that an air force officer was chosen to command the entire IDF.[4] Considered by many as vain and arrogant, Halutz possessed the utmost confidence in air power and precision weapons, going so far as to suggest in 2001 that the IDF needed "to part with the concept of a land battle" altogether.[5] Not surprisingly, Halutz endorsed a completely new doctrine for the IDF, one that relied heavily on EBO, SOD, and precision firepower-based operations at the expense of the ground maneuver forces.

The new doctrine was a departure from the traditional, in that emphasis was now placed on precision firepower as "magical 'game changing' systems." Halutz's adherence to the faulty new doctrine was made even more problematic by the inadequately prepared IDF ground forces.[6]

Israeli Major General Amiram Levin, a former northern army commander, wrote after the war that he thought the doctrine "was built around the genius of the commanding officer instead of placing emphasis upon proper staff work." He was also convinced that the new doctrine stood "in complete contradiction to the most important basic principles of operating an army in general and the IDF in particular. It is not based upon, and even ignores, the universal fundamentals of warfare. Moreover, the new concept disregards the uniqueness of the IDF and the development of military traditions. . . . This is not a concept that is better or worse. It is a completely mistaken concept that could not succeed and should never have been relied upon."[7]

One of the most critical indictments of Halutz, the IDF campaign plan, and the new EBO/SOD doctrine it was based on came from Haninah Levine, a science fellow at the Center for Defense Information, in his synopsis of the Winograd Commission Interim Report. Levine wrote that "as the conflict unfolded, Halutz's optimistic assessment of the military's state of readiness merged with his false confidence in the abilities of its advanced weapon systems . . . to create a state in which the chief of staff's concept of what his forces were capable of achieving was completely divorced both from reality and from what the information available to him suggested."[8]

Shimon Naveh's SOD, which formed the core of the new IDF doctrine, also proved highly disruptive. The new language and methodology severely handicapped many commanders in the field. A large majority of IDF officers simply did not grasp the SOD-inspired doctrine. When the terminology made its way into at least one division's operation orders, the brigade commanders were at a complete loss to understand them. The use of this effects-based, SOD-inspired doctrine in the 2006 Hezbollah-Israeli war should promote spirited debate within the US Military's doctrinal establishment and stand as a lucent example of the limitations of EBO.

Another crucial factor in the IDF's reverses in southern Lebanon was the dismal performance of its ground forces. Years of counterinsurgency (COIN) operations had seriously diminished its conventional warfighting capabilities. The IDF was completely dismayed to find that its land forces could not conduct a successful ground campaign in southern Lebanon. Although Naveh was heavily criticized, his observations are astute and timely. "The point is, the IDF fell in love with what it was doing with the Palestinians," he stated. "In fact it became addictive. You know when you fight a war against a rival who's by all means inferior to you, you may lose a guy here or there, but you're in total control. It's nice, you can pretend that you fight the war and yet it's not really a dangerous war. . . . I remember talking to five brigade commanders. . . . I asked them if they had an idea . . . what it meant to go into battle against a Syrian division? Did they have in mind what a barrage of 10 Syrian artillery battalions looked like?"[9]

In the conventional arena, the IDF ground forces performed unsatisfactorily. The fight at Wadi al-Saluki, for example, revealed the failure of tank commanders and crewmen to use their smokescreen systems, the lack of indirect-fire skills, and the total absence of combined arms proficiency.[10] The IDF lost many of these perishable combat skills during its long years of COIN operations against the Palestinians.

Hezbollah proved to be a highly dedicated and professional fighting force, armed with some of the most advanced weapon systems in the world. There can be no doubt that the IDF greatly underestimated its opponent. From 2000 to 2006, Hezbollah successfully embraced a new doctrine, transforming itself from a predominantly guerrilla force into a formidable quasi-conventional fighting force. Hezbollah correctly ascertained the manner in which the IDF would fight the war and prepared its resources and command and control systems to effectively withstand an EBO campaign.

In the tactical arena, Hezbollah proved a worthy adversary for IDF ground forces. Its use of swarming ATGMs and RPGs against Israeli tanks was both shrewd and inventive.[11] Of the 114 IDF personnel killed during the war, 30 were tank crewmen.[12] Out of the 400 tanks involved in the fighting in southern Lebanon, 48 were hit, 40 were damaged, and 20 penetrated. It is believed that five Merkavas were completely destroyed.[13] Clearly, Hezbollah has mastered the art of light infantry/ATGM tactics against heavy mechanized forces. Hezbollah also deserves high marks for its innovative use of sophisticated ambushes and the clever use of both direct and indirect fires.[14]

The lackluster performance of the IDF in the 2006 Hezbollah-Israeli war was the result of a multiplicity of factors. Halutz's steadfast confidence in air power, coupled with his disdain for land warfare, increased the strength of the IAF at the expense of the ground forces. While continuing COIN operations against the Palestinians, the IDF saw its budget for ground forces slashed and training for major combat operations by divisions and brigades greatly reduced. Within the IDF reserve, equipment was not replaced or repaired, and the tactical skills of both reserve and regular ground forces continued to decline. Training for reserve tank crewmen was all but forgotten.

The new Halutz doctrine served to compound the serious deficiencies inherent in the ground forces. The language and style incorporated in the doctrine proved nearly incomprehensible to many officers within the IDF. When air power proved ineffective in stopping Hezbollah's rocket attacks, Halutz was compelled to call upon his ground forces. Not surprisingly, they, too, proved to be unsuccessful.

It is apparent the US Army would do well to further examine the outcomes of the 2006 Hezbollah-Israeli war, especially as it relates to COIN, EBO, and SOD. While the US Army continues to perform irregular warfare operations throughout the world, it must not lose its ability to execute major combat operations. The results of this war do not call for an indictment of EBO per se but underscore the fact that they cannot be effective when used exclusive of ground maneuver operations. Shimon Naveh's SOD has come under much criticism for being nearly incomprehensible to those who were charged with its implementation. The core of SOD may not be without merit, but it is useless if it cannot be understood by officers attempting to carry out operation orders using SOD terminology and methodology.

The missteps committed by the IDF in this war provide the US Army with valuable examples of potential difficulties when counterinsurgency operations are abruptly changed to major combat operations. For the US Army, which has been almost exclusively involved in irregular warfare for years, this issue is of paramount importance. While the US Army must be proficient in conducting major combat operations around the world, it is possible that years of irregular operations have chipped away at this capability, not unlike the situation encountered by the IDF.

Notes

1. David Makovsky and Jeffrey White, "Lessons And Implications Of The Israeli-Hizballah War: A Preliminary Assessment," The Washington Institute for Near East Policy, Policy Focus No. 60 (October 2006), 43.

2. Ron Tira, "The Limitations Of Standoff Firepower-Based Operations: On Standoff Warfare, Maneuver, and Decision," *Institute for National Strategic Studies, Memorandum 89*, March 2007, 44.

3. Ron Tira, "Breaking The Amoeba's Bones," *Strategic Assessment*, Jaffee Center for Strategic Studies, Tel Aviv University Vol. 9, No. 3 (November 2006), 1-2, http://www.tau.ac.il/jcss/sa/v9n3p3Tira.html (accessed 10 September 2007).

4. The Chief of the General Staff Lieutenant General Dan Halutz was born in 1948 in Tel Aviv. He grew up in Moshav Hagor and completed his high school studies at the "Kogel" high school in Holon. Dan Halutz was drafted into the IDF in 1966, and volunteered for the IAF's pilot's course, which he completed in 1968 as a combat pilot. After completing a field training course on an "Oragon" plane and serving as a pilot on the "Mister 4" and "Vutour" planes, he transferred, at the end of 1969, to the IAF's first "Phantom" Squadron ("The One"). He then participated in the War of Attrition, during which he completed approximately 40 operational sorties, and after which he was posted as an instructor at the IAF flight school. In 1973, Dan Halutz was released from service in the IDF. He continued to serve as a reserve pilot, which included service in the Yom Kippur War, during which he completed 43 operational sorties. After the war, he returned to serve as executive officer of the "Phantom" Squadron. In 1978, Halutz was released from active duty once more and served as a reserve pilot for four years, during which he participated in operation "Peace for Galilee." In 1982, he returned to service and began piloting F-16 aircraft. In 1984, he received command over the "Phantom" Squadron, and two years later was appointed Head of the Operational Unit of the "Lavi" project. Dan Halutz's command positions in the IAF included Head of the Weapon Systems Department, Commander of the IAF Base "Hatzor," Head of the Air Division and Chief of the IAF Staff. He took part in the IAF's operational activities since the War of Attrition and acquired rich operational experience with hundreds of operational sorties, which resulted in the downing of three enemy aircraft. In July of 1998, Dan Halutz was promoted to the rank of Major General and appointed Assistant Head of the General Staff Branch in the IDF's General Staff. In April 2000, he was appointed Commander of the IAF. In July 2004, he was appointed Deputy Chief of the General Staff. In June 2005, Lieutenant General Halutz was appointed Chief of the IDF General Staff. During his service in the IAF, Halutz has accumulated approximately 4000 flight hours. Ron Tira, Private Collection.

5. Sarah E. Kreps, "The 2006 Lebanon War: Lessons Learned," *Parameters*, Spring 2007, 72-84, http://www.carlisle.army.mil/USAWC/Parameters/07spring/kreps.htm

6. "'The 'Revolution In Military Affairs' Shocks But Does Not Awe Israeli Commission," CDI Center For Defense Information, Straus Military Reform

Project, 11 June 2007, 1, http://www.cdi.org/friendlyversion/printversion.
cfm?documentID=3977 (accessed 10 September 2007).

7. Alex Fishman, B4.

8. "'The Revolution In Military Affairs' Shocks But Does Not Awe Israeli Commission," CDI Center For Defense Information, Straus Military Reform Project, 11 June 2007, http://www.cdi.org/friendlyversion/printversion. cfm?documentID=3977 (accessed 20 September 2007).

9. Shimon Naveh, interview by author, 1 November 2007.

10. Helmer, "Not Quite Counterinsurgency," 10-11.

11. Ibid, 11.

12. "Israel At War: 156 Dead," *Ynetnews.com*, 13 August 2006, http://www.ynetnews.com/articles/0,7340,L-3289147,00.html (accessed 14 October 2007).

13. Makovsky and White, 46.

14. Helmer, "Not Quite Counterinsurgency," 9.

Bibliography

Published Articles

Barnea, Nahum. "Israel vs. Hezbollah." *Foreign Policy,* November–December 2006.

Ben-David, Alon. "Lebanon War Report Reproaches Israeli Leaders." *Jane's Defence Weekly*, Vol. 44, No. 19, May 2007.

Boot, Max. "The Second Lebanon War." *Weekly Standard,* September 2006.

Gordon, Shmuel L. "The Vulture and the Snake: Counter-Guerrilla Air Warfare: The War in Southern Lebanon." *Mideast Security and Policy Studies*, No. 39, July 1998.

Helmer, Captain Daniel. "Not Quite Counterinsurgency: A Cautionary Tale for US Forces Based on Israel's Operation Change of Direction." *Armor,* January–February 2007.

Inbar, Efraim. "How Israel Bungled the Second Lebanon War." *Middle East Quarterly*, Summer 2007.

Kreps, Sarah E. "The 2006 Lebanon War: Lessons Learned." *Parameters*, Vol. XXXVII, No. 1, Spring 2007.

Murden, Simon, "Understanding Israel's Long Conflict in Lebanon: The Search for an Alternative Approach to Security During the Peace Process," *British Journal of Middle Eastern Studies*, Vol. 27, No. 1, May, 2000.

Nisan, Mordechai. "Did Israel Betray Its Lebanese Allies?" *Middle East Quarterly*, December, 2000.

Norton, Augustus Richard. "Hizballah and the Israeli Withdrawal from Southern Lebanon." *Journal of Palestine Studies*, Vol. 30, No. 1, Autumn 2000.

Norton, Augustus Richard and Jillian Schwedler. "(In)Security Zones in South Lebanon." *Journal of Palestine Studies*, Vol. 23, No. 1, Autumn 1993.

"North Koreans Assisted Hezbollah with Tunnel Construction." *Terrorism Focus*, Vol. 3, No. 30, August 2006.

Vego, Milan N. "Effects-Based Operations: A Critique." *JFQ*, No. 41, 2nd Quarter, 2006.

Wenger, Martha and Julie Denney. "Lebanon's Fifteen-Year War 1975–1990." *Middle East Report*, No. 162, January–February 1990.

Books

Achcar, Gilbert with Michel Warschawski. *The 33-Day War: Israel's War on Hezbollah in Lebanon and It's Consequences*. Boulder and London: Paradigm Publishers, 2007.

Campbell, Kenneth J. *A Tale of Two Quagmires: Iraq, Vietnam, and the Hard Lessons of War*. Boulder and London: Paradigm Publishers, 2007.

Chehabi, H.E. *Distant Relations: Iran and Lebanon in the last 500 years*. London: I.B. Tauris, 2006.

Clausewitz, Carl von. *On War*. Edited by Michael Howard and Peter Paret. Princeton, NJ: Princeton University Press, 1976.

Collelo, Thomas. *Lebanon: A Country Study*. Washington DC: Federal Research Division, Library of Congress, 1987.

69

Creveld, Martin van. *The Sword and the Olive: A Critical History of the Israeli Defense Force*. New York: Public Affairs, 1998.

Gabriel, Richard A. *Operation Peace for Galilee: The Israeli-PLO War in Lebanon*. New York: Hill and Wang, 1985.

Hamizrachi, Beate. *The Emergence of the South Lebanon Security Belt: Major Saad Haddad and the Ties with Israel, 1975–1978*. New York: Praeger, 1988.

Harik, Judith Palmer. *Hezbollah: The Changing Face of Terrorism*. London: I.B. Tauris, 2004.

Harmon, Adam. *Lonely Soldier: The Memoir of an American Soldier in the Israeli Army*. New York: Ballantine Books, 2006.

Harris, William W. *Faces of Lebanon: Sects, Wars, and Global Extensions*. Princeton, NJ: Markus Wiener Publishers, 1997.

Helmer, Daniel Isaac. *Flipside of the COIN: Israel's Lebanese Incursion Between 1982–2000. The Long War Series Occasional Paper 21*. Fort Leavenworth, KS: Combat Studies Institute Press, 2006.

Laffin, John. *The War of Desperation: Lebanon 1982–85*. London: Osprey, 1985.

Noe, Nicholas, ed., *Voice of Hezbollah: The Statements of Sayyed Hassan Nasrallah*, London: Verso, 2007.

Norton, Augustus Richard. *Amal and the Shi'a: Struggle for the Soul of Lebanon*. Austin: University of Texas Press, 1987.

Norton, Augustus Richard. *Hezbollah: A Short History*. Princeton and Oxford: Princeton University Press, 2007.

Qassem, Naim. *Hizbullah: The Story from Within*. Translated by Dalia Khalil. London: SAQI, 2005.

Schiff, Zeev. *A History of the Israeli Army 1874 To The Present*. New York: Macmillan Publishing Company, 1985.

Shelah, Ofer and Yaov Limor. *Captives In Lebanon*. Miskal, Yedioth Ahrononth and Chemed Books, 2007. (Hebrew)

Smith, Edward A. *Effects Based Operations: Applying Network Centric Warfare in Peace, Crisis, and War*. Washington DC: The Command and Control Research Program, 2002.

Internet Sources

"9 IDF Troops Killed in Day of Fighting." *Ynetnews.com*. http://www.ynetnews.com/articles/0,7340,L-3281856,00.html (accessed 4 October 2007).

Amman, Khalil Marwan in. "Hizbullah Vows to Fight on as Israel Prepares Retreat from Lebanon." *Crescent International* (May 2000). http://www.muslimedia.com/archives/oaw00/leb-kidnap.htm (accessed 15 July 2007).

Amos, Harel. "Army Inquiries Into Lebanon War Will Lead to Personnel Changes." *Haaretz.com*. http://www.haaretz.com/hasen/spages/772276.html (accessed 15 June 2007).

"Arab Assessments of the War in Lebanon." *Intelligence and Terrorism Information Center at the Israel Intelligence Heritage & Commemoration Center (IICC).*

http://www.terrorism-info.org.il/site/html/search.asp?sid=13&pid=161&nu mResults=3&isSearch=yes&isT8=yes (accessed 21 August 2007).

Ariel, Jonathan. "Analysis: Government and IDF Racked by Unprecedented Leadership Crisis." *Israelinsider*. http://web.israelinsider.com/bin/en.jsp?en DispWho=Article%E19 (accessed 21 June 2007).

Bangash, Zafar. "Hizbullah, the Party of God, Puts the Fear of God in the Followers of Satan." *Muslimedia* (October 1997). http://www.muslimedia. com/archives/special98/hizbulah.htm (accessed 25 July 2007).

Bar-Joseph, Uri. "Their Most Humiliating Hour." *Bint Jbeil*. http://www.bintjbeil. com/articles/2007/en/0427-barjoseph.html (accessed 16 June 2007).

Bart, Roni. "The Second Lebanon War: The Plus Column." *Strategic Assessment*. Jaffee Center for Strategic Studies, Tel Aviv University. http://www.tau.ac.il/ jcss/sa/v9n3p4Bart.html (accessed 1 August 2007).

Ben-David, Alon. "Hizbullah Hits Israel's INS Hanit with Anti-ship Missile." *Jane's Defence News* (July 2006). http://www.janes.com/defence/news/jdw/ jdw060718_1_n.shtml (accessed 20 June 2007).

Bentsur, Eytan. "Op-ed Article on Israel's Withdrawal from Lebanon." *Israel Ministry of Foreign Affairs* (May 2000). http://www.israel-mfa.gov.il/MFA/ Government/Speeches+by+Israeli+leaders/2000/Op-ed+Article+on+Israel- s+Withdrawal+from+Lebanon.html (accessed 21 June 2007).

Berkovich, Dani. "Doesn't Hizbollah Brake at Red Lights?" *Strategic Assessment*. Jaffee Center for Strategic Studies, Tel Aviv University. Vol. 9, No. 4 (March 2007). http://www.tau.ac.il/jcss/sa/9_4_02.html (accessed 10 June 2007).

"Bint Jbeil: Hezbollah Heartland." *BBC News*. http://news.bbc.co.uk/2/hi/middle_ east/5221086.stm (accessed 19 September 2007).

Bishara, Marwan. "America's Asymmetrical Wars: Following a Failed Israeli Military Doctrine." *For The Record, The Jerusalem Fund*. http://www. thejerusalemfund.org/images/fortherecord.php?ID=21 (accessed 12 June 2007).

Catignani, Sergio. "The Israeli-Hezbollah Rocket War: A Preliminary Assessment." *Global Strategy Forum* (September 2006). www.globalstrategyforum.org (accessed 1 August 2007).

Cody, Edward and Molly Moore. "The Best Guerrilla Force in the World: Analysts Attribute Hezbollah's Resilience to Zeal, Secrecy and Iranian Funding." *Washingtonpost.com*. http://www.wahingtonpost.com/wp-dyn/ content/article/2006/08/13/AR2006081300719_pf (accessed 1 July 2007).

"Commander of IDF Lebanon-Liaison Unit Killed, Warrant Officer, Soldier, and Civilian Killed in Explosion." *Israel Ministry of Foreign Affairs*. http://www. mfa.gov.il/MFA/Government/Communiques/1999/Commander%20of%2 0IDF%20Lebanon-Liaison%20Unit%20and%20Three%20Ot (accessed 1 August 2007).

Creveld, Martin van. "How the Victorious IDF of 1967 Become the Defeated IDF of 2006." *JewishJournal.com*. http://www.jewishjournal.com/home/preview. php?id=17745 (accessed 27 February 2008).

Crooke, Alastair and Mark Perry. "How Hezbollah Defeated Israel, Part 1: Winning the Intelligence War." *Asia Times Online.* http://www.atimes.com/atimes/Middle_East/HJ12AK01.html (accessed 29 June 2007).

Crooke, Alastair and Mark Perry. "How Hezbollah Defeated Israel, Part 2: Winning the Ground War." *Asia Times Online.* http://www.atimes.com/atimes/Middle_East/HJ13AK01.html (accessed 14 June 2007).

"Deadly Battles in Bint Jbeil: Fallen Soldiers' Stories." *Ynetnews.com.* http://www.ynetnews.com/articles/0,7340,L-3282017,00.html (accessed 4 October 2007).

"Deconstructing Hizbullah's Surprise Military Prowess." *Jane's Intelligence Review* (November 2006). http://www4.janes.com/subscribe/jir/doc_view.jsp?K2DocKey=/content1/janesdata/mags/jir/history/jir2006/jir10050.htm@current&Prod_Name=JIR&QueryText (accessed 15 June 2007).

Derfner, Larry. "Lambs to the Slaughter?" *Jerusalem Post Online Edition* (August 2006). http://www.jpost.com/servlet/Satellite?cid=1154525936658&pagename=JPost/JPArticle/ShowFull (accessed 15 October 2007).

Erlich, Reuven. "Agreements, Arrangements and Understandings Concerning Lebanon to Which Israel was Involved During the Past 30 Years – Background, Data, Lessons and Conclusions." *Intelligence and Terrorism Information Center at the Israel Intelligence Heritage & Commemoration Center (IICC)* (No Date). http://www.terrorism-info.org.il/site/html/search.asp?sid=13&pid=161&numResults=5&isSearch=yes&isT8=yes (accessed 21 august 2007).

Erlich, Reuven. "Hezbollah's Use of Lebanese Civilians as Human Shields: The extensive military infrastructure positioned and hidden in populated areas. From within the Lebanese towns and villages deliberate rocket attacks were directed against civilian targets in Israel." *Intelligence and Terrorism Information Center at the Israel Intelligence Heritage & Commemoration Center (IICC).* http://www.terrorism-info.org.il/site/html/search.asp?sid=13&pid=161&numResults=2&isSearch=yes&isT8=yes (accessed 21 August 2007).

Erlich, Reuven. "Raising the issue of the Shebaa's Farms in proposed American-French Security Council draft resolution for ending the fighting: background information and significance." *Intelligence and Terrorism Information Center at the Israel Intelligence Heritage & Commemoration Center (IICC).* http://www.terrorism-info.org.il/site/html/search.asp?sid=13&pid=161&numResults=4&isSearch=yes&isT8=yes *(accessed 21 August 2007).*

Eshel, David. "Hezbollah's Intelligence War." *Defense Update.* http//www.defense-update.com/analysis/Lebanon_war_1.html (accessed 14 June 2007).

Eshel, David. "Is Israel Victimizing Itself by its Own Openness?" *Defense Update.* http//www.defense-update.com/analysis_130507_self_victimizing_democracy.htm (accessed 19 June 2007).

"High-ranking Officers Didn't Undergo Training for Their Positions." *European Jewish Congress. Israeli Press Review* (May 2006). http://www.eurojewcong.org/ejc/news.php?id_article=641 (accessed 15 June 2007).

Fendel, Hillel. "Retiring General: Disengagement Led to IDF Failure in Lebanon." *Arutz Sheva IsraelNationalNews.com.* http.www.israelnationalnews.com.

Finer, Jonathan. "Israeli Soldiers Find a Tenacious Foe in Hezbollah," *WashingtonPost.com* (August 2006). http://www.washingtonpost.com/wp-dyn/content/article/2006/08/07/AR2006080701453.html (accessed 9 October 2007).

Fishman, Alex. "The Changing Face of the IDF: The Security Agenda and the Ballot Box." *Strategic Assessment*. Jaffee Center for Strategic Studies, Vol. 8, No. 4 (February 2006). http://www.tau.ac.il/jcss/sa/v8n4p3Fishman.html (accessed 25 September 2007).

"General Blames Halutz for War Failure." *Ynetnews.com*. http://www.ynetnews.com/Ext/Comp/ArticleLayout/CdaArticleprin (accessed 5 June 2007).

Hanan, Greensberg. "Commander: Egoz Must Keep Fighting." *Ynetnews.com*. http://www.ynetnews.com/articles/0,7340,L-3279381,00.html.

Harel, Amos. "Caught Between the Pride of Combat and the Public's Criticism." *Haaretz.com*. http//www.haaretz.com/hasen/spages/783040.html (accessed 16 June 2007).

Harel, Amos. "Seven Months On, IDF Implementing Lessons of Lebanon War." *Haaretz.com*. http://www.haaretz.com/hasen/spages/822989.html (accessed 1 August 2007).

Harel, Amos and Amir Oren. "Halutz Appoints Team to Examine Hezbollah Kidnapping of Soldiers." *Haaretz.com*. http://www.haaretz.com/hasen/spages/764384.html (accessed 17 September 2007).

Hasson, Nir. "Gal Hirsch: MI Warning Would Have Prevented Soldiers' Abduction." *Haaretz.com*. http://www.haaretz.com/hasen/spages/788306.html (accessed 12 July 2007).

Hasson, Nir and Aluf Benn. "PM to War Probe: IDF Let Itself Down in Second Lebanon War." *Haaretz.com*. http://www.haaretz.com/hasen/spages/858071.html (accessed 21 June 2007).

Hazony, David. "The War of Fog." *Azure*. http//www.azure.org.il/magazine/popup_print.asp?ID=332&member_ID= (accessed 6 July 2007).

Heller, Aron. "Lebanon Offensive Criticized in Israel," *Washingtonpost.com* (July 2006). http://www.washingtonpost.com/wp-dyn/content/article/2006/07/26/AR2006072601156_pf.html (accessed 1 October 2007).

Heller, Mark A. "Implications of the Withdrawal from Lebanon For Israeli-Palestinian Relations." *Strategic Assessment*. Jaffee Center for Strategic Studies, Tel Aviv University. Vol. 3, No. 1 (June 2000). http://www.tau.ac.il/jcss/sa/v3n1p6.html (accessed 17 July 2007).

Hendel, Yoaz. "Failed Tactical Intelligence in the Lebanon War." *Strategic Assessment*. Jaffee Center for Strategic Studies, Tel Aviv University. Vol. 9, No. 3 (November 2006). http://www.tau.ac.il/jcss/sa/v9n3p9Hendel.html (accessed 1 July 2007).

"Hezbollah a North Korea-Type Guerilla Force." *Intelligence Online* (August – September 2006). www.IntelligenceOnline.com (accessed 21 August 2007).

"Hezbollah as a case study of the battle for hearts and minds in the confrontation between Israel and the terrorist organizations." *Intelligence and Terrorism Information Center at the Israel Intelligence Heritage & Commemoration Center (IICC)*. http://www.terrorism-info.org.il/site/html/search.asp?sid=1

3&pid=161&numResults=4&isSearch=yes&isT8=yes (accessed 21 August 2007).

"Hezbollah as a Strategic Arm of Iran." *Intelligence and Terrorism Information Center at the Israel Intelligence Heritage & Commemoration Center (IICC)* (September 2006). http://www.terrorism-info.org.il/site/html/search.asp?sid=13&pid=161&numResults=4&isSearch=yes&isT8=yes (accessed 21 August 2007).

"Hezbollah Kills 8 Soldiers, Kidnaps Two in Offensive on Northern Border," *Haaretz.com*, (July 2006). http://www.haaretz.com/hasen/pages/ShArt.jhtml?itemNo=737825 (accessed 18 September 2007).

"Hizbullah Attacks Along Israel's Northern Border May 2000-June 2006." *Israel ministry of Foreign Affairs* (June 2006). http://www.mfa.gov.il/NR/exeres/9EE216D7-82EF-4274-B80D-6BBD1803E8A7,frameless.htm?NRMODE=Published (accessed 20 August 2007).

"Hizbullah's Katyusha Rockets Force Barak to Back Down." *Crescent International* (May 2000). http://www.muslimedia.com/archives/world00/katyusha.htm (accessed 12 July 2007).

Howland, Jonathan. "IDF Shake-UP Over Hezbollah War." *The Jewish Institute for National Security Affairs (March 2007).* http://www.jinsa.org/articles/print.htm/documentid/3736 (accessed 5 July 2007).

Human Rights Watch. "The Occupied Zone: An Overview." http://www.hrw.org/reports/1999/lebanon/Isrlb997-02.htm (accessed 12 February 2008).

"IDF Spokesman: Hizbullah Attack on Northern Border and IDF Response." *Israel Ministry of Foreign Affairs* (July 2006). http://www.mfa.gov.il/MFA/Terrorism-+Obstacle+to+Peace/Terrorism+from+Lebanon-+Hizbullah/Hizbullah+attack+on+northern+border+and+IDF+response+12-Jul-2006.htm (accessed 18 September 2007).

"Israeli Army in Race Against a UN Ceasefire in Lebanon." *DEBKAfile.* http://wwwdebka.com/article_print.php?aid=1200 (accessed 5 June 2007).

"Israeli General Killed in Lebanon." *BBC Online Network.* http://news.bbc.co.uk/1/hi/world/middle_east/287941.stm (accessed 1 August 2007).

Katz, Yaakov. "Commanders Failed to Fulfill Missions." *Jerusalem Post Online Edition* (October 2006). http://www.jpost.com/servlet/Satellite?cid=1159193446682&pagename=JPost%2FJPArticle%2FShowFull (accessed 11 October 2007).

Katz, Yaakov. "Names of Nine Soldiers Killed in Lebanon Released," *Jerusalem Post,* http://info.jpost.com/C002/Supplements/CasualtiesOfWar/2006_07_26.html (accessed 4 October 2007).

Keegan, John. "Why Israel Will Go to War Again–Soon." *Telegraph.co.uk.* http://www.telegraph.co.uk/opinion/main.jhtml?xml=/opinion/2006/11/03/do0302.xml (accessed 6 July 2007).

Kulick, Amir. "Hizbollah vs. the IDF: The Operational Dimension." *Strategic Assessment,* Vol. 9, No. 3 (November 2006). http://www.tau.ac.il/jcss/sa/v9n3p7Kulick.html (accessed 15 July 2007).

Myre, Greg. "Risks Escalate as Israel Fights a Ground War." *The New York Times* (August 2006), http://www.nytimes.com/2006/08/05/world/middleeast/ 05zone.html (accessed 1 October 2007).

Nahal Haredi-Netzah Yehuda Battalion. "7/17/2006 Nahal Haredi Soldiers in Lebanon." http://www.nahalharedi.org/nahal_haredi_news.php?id=26 (accessed 6 June 2007).

Noe, Nicholas. "A Response to Andrew Exum's "Hizbollah at War: A Military Assessment,*"* 5. http://64.233.167.104/search?q=cache:CYqBLHuWCV8J: www.mideastwire.com/downloads/Response%2520to%2520Andrew%2520 Exum.pdf+%22a+response+to+andrew+exum%27s+%22Hizbollah+at+war &hl=en&ct=clnk&cd=1&gl=us *(accessed 21 August 2006).*

"Operation Accountability." *Ynetnews.com* (August 2006). http://www.ynetnews. com/articles/0,7340,L-3284732,00.html (accessed 12 August 2007).

"Operation Grapes of Wrath." *Ynetnews.com* (August 2006). http://www. ynetnews.com/articles/0,7340,L-3284744,00.html (accessed 10 August 2007).

Ophir, Noam. "Look Not to the Skies: The IAF vs. Surface-to-Surface Rocket Launchers." *Strategic Assessment*. Jaffee Center for Strategic Studies, Tel Aviv University, Vol. 9. No.3 (November 2006). http://www.tau.ac.il/jcss/sa/ v9n3p5Ophir.html (accessed 5 August 2007).

Oren, Amir. "Analysis: In Lebanon, Government Hamstrung Troubled Division." *Haaretz.com*. http://www.haaretz.com/hasen/spages/774974.html (accessed 1 July 2007).

Osman, Khalil. "The Key Elements of the Victory of the Hizbullah-led Islamic Resistance in Southern Lebanon." *Crescent International* (July 2000). http:// www.muslimedia.com/ARCHIVES/oaw00/hizb-key.htm

Pfeffer, Anshel. "After Maron al-Ras Battle Bint-Jbail Looms as Next Challenge." *Jerusalem Post* (July 2006). http://www.jpost.com/servlet/Satellite?cid=115 3291981228&pagename=JPost%2FJPArticle%2FShowFull (accessed 25 September 2007).

Pfeffer, Anshel. "It Was All So Very Fast-The Shooting, The Shouting." *Jerusalem Post Online Edition*. (July 2007). http://www.jpost.com/servlet/Satellite?cid =1153292016359&pagename=JPost%2FJPArticle%2FPrinter (accessed 4 October 2007).

"Press Release SC/6878." *United Nations*. http://www.un.org/News/Press/ docs/2000/20000618.sc6878.doc.html (accessed 22 August 2007).

Prothero, Mitchell. "The Day Israel Realized That This Was a Real War." *Guardian Unlimited*. (July 2006). http://observer.guardian.co.uk/world/ story/0,,1833349,00.html (accessed 4 October 2007).

"Secret Meeting." *Ynetnews.com* (March 2007). http://www.ynetnews.com/ articles/0,7340,L-3383151,00.html (accessed 12 July 2007).

"Secret Report: Chances Captive Survived Are Slim." *Ynetnews.com*. http://www. ynetnews.com/articles/0,7340,L-3401556,00.html (accessed 17 September 2007).

"Security Council Calls For End To Hostilities Between Hizbollah, Israel," United Nations Security Council SC/8808 (August 2006). http://www.un.org/News/ Press/docs/2006/sc8808.doc.htm (accessed 10 October 2007).

Shalom, Zaki and Yoaz Hendel. "Conceptual Flaws on the Road to the Second Lebanon War." *Strategic Assessment*. Jaffee Center for Strategic Studies, Tel Aviv University, Vol. 10, No. 1 (June 2007). http://www.tau.ac.il/jcss/sa/10_1_05.html (accessed 27 August 2007)

Shapira, Shimon Brig. Gen. "Countdown to Conflict: Hizballah's Military Buildup and the Need for Effective Disarmament." *Intelligence and Terrorism Information Center at the Israel Intelligence Heritage & Commemoration Center (IICC). http://www.terrorism-info.org.il/site/html/search.asp?sid=1 3&pid=161&numResults=4&isSearch=yes&isT8=yes* (accessed 21 August 2007).

Shatz, Adam. "Nasrallah's Game." *The Nation*. http://www.thenation.com/docprint.mhtml?i=20060731&s=nasrallah_game (accessed 6 June 2007).

Siboni, Gabriel. "Command in the IDF." *Strategic Assessment*. Jaffee Center for Strategic Studies, Tel Aviv University, Vol. 9, No.4 (March 2007). http://www.tau.ac.il/jcss/sa/v9n3p5Ophir.html (accessed 11 July 2007).

Tira, Ron. "Breaking the Amoeba's Bones." *Strategic Assessment* Vol. 9, No. 3 (November 2006). http://www.tau.ac.il/jcss/sa/v9n3p3Tira.html (accessed 15 June 2007).

"The Israeli Military is in a Crisis of Leadership." *Spiegel Online*. http://www.spiegel.de/international/0,1518,449793,00.html (accessed 20 August 2007).

"The Israeli Withdrawal From Southern Lebanon." *Jewish Virtual Library*. http://www.jewishvirtuallibrary.org/jsource/Peace/lebwith.html (accessed 1 August 2007).

"The Israeli Withdrawal from Southern Lebanon-Special Update." *Israel Ministry of Foreign Affairs* (May 2000). http://www.israel-mfa.gov.il/MFA/History/Modern+History/Historic+Events/The+Israeli+Withdrawal+from+Southern+Lebanon-+Spec.htm (accessed 12 August 2007).

"The Occupied Zone: An Overview." http://www.hrw.org/reports/1999/lebanon/Isrlb997-02.htm (accessed 5 August 2007).

"The Winograd Report." *Haaretz.com.* http://www.haaretz.com/hasen/spages/854051.html (accessed 5 July 2007).

"United Nations Interim Force in Lebanon." *Peace and Security Section of the Department of Information in cooperation with the Department of Peacekeeping Operations, United Nations.* http://www.un.org/Depts/dpko/missions/unifil/background.html (accessed 22 August 2007).

"Using the Quds Force of the Revolutionary Guards as the main tool to export the revolution beyond the borders of Iran." *Intelligence and Terrorism Information Center at the Israel Intelligence Heritage & Commemoration Center (IICC)* (April 2007). http://www.terrorism-info.org.il/site/html/search.asp?sid=13&pid=167&numResults=2&isSearch=yes&isT8=yes (accessed 21 August 2007).

"War was a Catastrophe, Top Security Officials Told Olmert." *Ynetnews.com*. http://www.ynetnews.com/articles/0,7340,L-3383151,00.html (accessed 15 July 2007).

Wegman, Yehuda. "Anti-War:" Has the IDF Really Lost Its Ability to Win Wars?" *Strategic Assessment*. Jaffee Center for Strategic Studies, Tel Aviv University, Vol. 9, No.4 (March 2007). http://www.tau.ac.il/jcss/sa/9_4_12.html (accessed 1 August 2007).

Winston, Emanuel A. "Making Israel Bleed." *Winston Mideast Analysis & Commentary* (March 1999). http://gamla.org.il/english/article/1999/march/win1.htm (accessed 1 August 2007).

Yehoshua, Yossi. "Lebanon War Commander Resigns." *Ynetnews.com.*

Ze'evi Aharon (Farkash). "A critical Look at Intelligence." *Strategic Assessment*. Jaffee Center for Strategic Studies, Tel Aviv University, Vol. 9, No. 4 (March 2007). http://www.tau.ac.il/jcss/sa/9_4_08.html (accessed 29 June 2007).

Newspapers

Avner, Yehuda. "A Battalion Commander's Anger." *The Jerusalem Post*, 22 August 2006.

Bar-Joseph, Uri. "Their Most Humiliating Hour." *Haaretz*, 27 April 2007.

Blanford, Nicholas, Daniel McGrory and Stephen Farrell. "Tactics Having Kept Israeli Army at Bay." *The Times*, 8 August 2006.

Blanford, Nicholas. "Hizbullah's resilience built on years of homework: Meticulous planning and a through understanding of Israeli military doctrine both play into its success." *The Christian Science Monitor*, 11 August 2006.

Cambanis, Thanassis. "Hezbollah Fighter Strove to be a Martyr." *The Boston Globe*, 30 December 2006.

Derfner, Larry. "Lambs to the slaughter." *The Jerusalem Post*, 24 August 2006.

"Eight IDF Soldiers Killed, 2 Kidnapped on Northern Frontier." *Jerusalem Post*, 12 July 2006.

Fishman, Alex. "Struck by a Virus." *Yedioth Ahronoth*, No Date.

Fisk, Robert. "Smoke Signals From The Battle of Bint Jbeil Send A Warning To Israel." *The Independent*, 27 June 2007.

Glick, Caroline. "Column One: Halutz's Stalinist Movement." *The Jerusalem Post*, 8 June 2006.

Goldenberg, Suzanne. "Chaos and Humiliation as Israel Pulls Out of Lebanon." *The Guardian*, 24 May 2000.

Goldenberg, Suzanne. "Israel Pulls Out: Last Troops Slam the Gate on Lebanon's Party." *The Guardian*, 25 May 2000.

Goldenberg, Suzanne. "Israel Pulls Out: SLA Exodus: Refugees Pour Over Frontier." *The Guardian*, 24 May 2000.

Himelfarb, Joel. "Hezbollah's Deadly Record." *The Washington Times*, 16 March 2005.

Horan, Deborah. "Israeli Forces Flee Positions in Lebanon." *Houston Chronicle*, 24 May 2000.

"Human Rights Watch Comes Under Fire from Hezbollah Over Report Critical of Guerrilla Group." *International Herald Tribune*, 29 August 2007.

Landau, David. "Israel Lays Groundwork for Withdrawal from Lebanon." *Jewish Telegraphic Agency*, No date.

"Israel Ends S. Lebanon Occupation; Muslim Guerrillas Swiftly Fill Void Early Withdrawal was Forced by Collapse of Allied Militia." *St. Louis Post-Dispatch*, 24 May 2000.

"Israel's Occupation of S. Lebanon Collapses." *St. Louis Post-Dispatch*, 23 May 2000.

"Israel Pulls Last Troops Out Of Lebanon Hezbollah Forces Move Into Border Positions." *Times Picayune*, 24 May 2000.

Katz, Yaakov. "IDF Report Card." *The Jerusalem Post*, 24 August 2006.

Katz, Yaakov. "Post-Battle Probe Finds Merkava Tank Misused in Lebanon." *Jerusalem Post*, 3 September 2006.

Katz, Yaakov. "Wadi Saluki Battle-Microcosm of the War's Mistakes." *The Jerusalem Post*, 29 August 2006.

Levins, Harry. "Israel Appears Glad to Be Free of Entanglements in Lebanon." *St. Louis Post-Dispatch*, 30 May 2000.

Mahnaimi, Uzi. "Humbling of the Supertroops Shatters Israeli Army Morale." *The Sunday Times,* 27 August 2006.

Rabinovich, Abraham. "Despite Ragtag Pullout From Lebanon, Israel is No Paper Tiger." *International Herald Tribune*, 30 May 2000.

Schiff, Ze'ev. "The Foresight Saga." *Haaretz*, 16 August 2006.

Schneider, Howard. "Israel's Army Is Gone, So Where Is Lebanon's?" *The Washington Post*, 8 June 2000.

Sontag, Deborah. "Israel Hurries Pullout Plans After Clashes Along Border." *The New York Times,* 9 May 2000.

Susser, Leslie. "Closing Ranks." *The Jerusalem Report*, 8 January 2007.

Susser, Leslie. "No more 'Post-Heroic' Warfare." *Jewish Telegraphic Agency*, 9 February 2007.

Tzuriel, Nava and Eitan Glickman. Translated by Adam Keller. "The Canyon of Death." *Yediot Aharonot*, 16 August 2006.

Whitaker, Brian. "Analysis: Withdrawal is at Best a Leap in the Dark." *The Guardian*, 6 May 2000.

Reports

Berkovich, Dani. "Doesn't Hizbollah Brake at Red Lights?" *Strategic Assessment* Jaffee Center for Strategic Studies, Vol. 9, No.4, March 2007.

"The Hezbollah Challenge: An Alternate Paradigm?" Assistant Deputy Chief of Staff for Intelligence, US Army Training and Doctrine Command, Fort Monroe, VA.

Cordesman, Anthony H. "Preliminary 'Lessons' of the Israeli-Hezbollah War." *Center for Strategic and International Studies*. Revised: 17 August 2006.

Exum, Andrew. *Hizballah at War: A Military Assessment. The Washington Institute for Near East Policy*. Policy Focus No. 63, December 2006.

Gordon, Shmuel L. "The Vulture and The Snake Counter-Guerrilla Air Warfare: The War in Southern Lebanon." *Mideast Security and Policy Studies*. Begin-Sadat Center for Strategic Studies. No. 39, July 1998.

Hendel, Yoaz. "Failed Tactical Intelligence in the Lebanon War." *Strategic Assessment, Jaffee Center for Strategic Studies*. Vol. 9, No. 3, November 2006.

Kober, Avi, "The Second Lebanon War." *Perspectives: The Begin-Sadat Center for Strategic Studies*. Perspectives Paper No. 22, 28 September 2006.

Levine, Haninah. "'The Revolution in Military Affairs' Shocks but Does Not Awe Israeli Commission." *Center For Defense Information, Straus Military Reform Project*. 11 June 2007.

Makovsky, David and White, Jeffrey. "Lessons and Implications of the Israel-Hizballah War: A Preliminary Assessment." *The Washington Institute for Near East Policy*. Policy Focus No. 60, October 2006.

Perthes, Volker. "Syria's Involvement in Lebanon." *Middle East Report*. No. 203, Spring 1997.

Reilly, James A. "Israel in Lebanon, 1975-82." *MERIP Reports*. No. 108–109, September-October 1982.

Russell, Tom. "A Lebanon Primer." *MERIP Reports*. No. 133, June 1985.

Sharp, Jeremy M. "Israel-Hamas-Hezbollah: The Current Conflict." *CRS Report for Congress, Congressional Research Service, The Library of Congress*, 21 July 2006.

Siboni, Gabriel. "Command in the IDF." *Strategic Assessment, Jaffee Center for Strategic Studies*, Vol.9, No. 4, March 2007.

"Thoughts On The Operational Art." *United States Marine Corps Marine Corps Warfighting Laboratory*, Marine Corps Combat Development Command, 11 October 2006.

Tira, Ron. "The Limitations of Standoff Firepower-Based Operations: On Standoff Warfare, Maneuver, and Decision." *Institute for National Strategic Studies*. Memorandum 89, March 2007.

Ze'evi, Aharon. "A Critical Look at Intelligence." *Strategic Assessment* Jaffee Center for Strategic Studies. Vol. 9, No. 4, March 2007.

Interviews

Ariely, Dr. Gil. Interview by author 22 June 2006.

Eiran, Ehud. E-mail interview by author 25 July, 5, 7 August 2007.

Naveh, Shimon. Interview by author 1 November 2006.

Tira, Ron. E-mail interview by author, 19, 20, 21 June, 15 August 2007.

Thesis

Acosta, David. *The Makara of Hizballah: Deception in the 2006 Summer War*. Monterey, California: Naval Post Graduate School, June 2007.

Whitting, Major Christopher E. *When David Became Goliath*. Fort Leavenworth, KS: US Army Command and General Staff College, 2001.

Appendix A

Final Report of the Commission to Investigate
the Lebanon Campaign*
(The Winograd Report)

January 30, 2008

<u>Press Release</u>

Good Evening.

1. About an hour ago we submitted the Final Report of the Commission to Investigate the Lebanon Campaign in 2006 to the Prime minister, Mr. Ehud Olmert, and to the Minister of Defense, Mr. Ehud Barak.

2. The task given to us was difficult and complex. It involved the examination of events in 34 days of fighting, and the scrutiny of events before the war, since the IDF had left Lebanon in 2000. This covered extensive, charged and complex facts, unprecedented in any previous Commission of Inquiry.

3. The fact that the Government of Israel opted for such an examination, and that the army conducted a large number of inquires of a variety of military events, are a sign of strength, and an indication that the political and military leaders of Israel are willing to expose themselves to critical review and to painful but required mending.

4. We have included in the classified version of the Report all the relevant facts we have found concerning the 2nd Lebanon war, systematically and in a chronological order.

*Information and Internet Department, Winograd Committee Final Report,
Israel Ministry of Foreign Affairs, 30 January 2008.

This presentation of the factual basis was an important part of our work. It is reasonable to assume that no single decision maker had access to a similar factual basis. In this task we had a unique advantage over others who have written about this war, since we had access to a lot of primary and comprehensive material, and the opportunity to clarify the facts by questioning many witnesses, commanders and soldiers, including bereaved families.

5. For obvious reasons, the unclassified Report does not include the many facts that cannot be revealed for reasons of protecting the state's security and foreign affairs. We tried, nonetheless, to balance between the wish to present the public with a meaningful picture of the events and the needs of security. We should note that we did not take the mere fact that some data has already been published in the media as a reason for including it in our unclassified Report.

6. We, the members of the Commission, acted according to the main objectives for which the Commission was established – to respond to the bad feelings of the Israeli public of a crisis and disappointment caused by the results of the 2nd Lebanon war, and from the way it was managed by the political and military echelons; and the wish to draw lessons from the failings of the war and its flaws, and to repair what is required, quickly and resolutely. We regarded as most important to investigate deeply what had happened, as a key to drawing lessons for the future, and their implementation.

7. This conception of our role was one of the main reasons for our decision not to include in the Final Report personal conclusions and recommendations. We believe that the primary need for improvements applies to the structural and systemic malfunctioning revealed in the war – on all levels.

Nonetheless, it should be stressed that the fact we refrained from imposing personal responsibility does not imply that no such responsibility exists. We also wish to repeat our statement from the Interim Report: We will not impose different standards of responsibility to the political and the military echelons, or to persons of different ranks within them.

8.   Let us emphasize: when we imposed responsibility on a system, an echelon or a unit, we did not imply that the responsibility was only or mainly of those who headed it at the time of the war. Often, such responsibility stemmed from a variety of factors outside the control of those at the head. In addition, a significant part of the responsibility for the failures and flaws we have found lies with those who had been in charge of preparedness and readiness in the years before the war.

9.   The purpose of this press release is not to sum up the Final Report. Rather, it is to present its highlights. The Report itself includes discussions of many important issues, which are an inseparable part of the Report, its conclusions and recommendations.

10.   In the Final Report we dealt mainly with the events of the period after the initial decision to go to war, which we had discussed in the Interim Report. Yet the events of the period covered by the Final Report took place under the shadow of the constraints created by the decision to go to war, with all its failings and flaws.

     We want to stress that we stand behind everything we said in the Interim Report, and the two parts of the Report complement each other.

11.   Overall, we regard the 2nd Lebanon war as a serious missed opportunity. Israel initiated a long war, which ended without its clear military victory. A semi-military organization of a few thousand men resisted, for a few weeks, the strongest army in the Middle East, which enjoyed full air superiority and size and technology advantages. The barrage of rockets aimed at Israel's civilian population lasted throughout the war, and the IDF did not provide an effective response to it. The fabric of life under fire was seriously disrupted, and many civilians either left their home temporarily or spent their time in shelters. After a long period of using only standoff fire power and limited ground activities, Israel initiated a large scale ground offensive, very close to the Security Council resolution imposing a cease fire. This offensive did not result in military gains and was not completed. These facts had

far-reaching implications for us, as well as for our enemies, our neighbors, and our friends in the region and around the world.

12. In the period we examined in the Final Report - from July 18, 2006, to August 14, 2006- again troubling findings were revealed, some of which had already been mentioned in the Interim Report:

- We found serious failings and shortcomings in the decision making processes and staff-work in the political and the military echelons and their interface.

- We found serious failings and flaws in the quality of preparedness, decision-making and performance in the IDF high command, especially in the Army.

- We found serious failings and flaws in the lack of strategic thinking and planning, in both the political and the military echelons.

- We found severe failings and flaws in the defence of the civilian population and in coping with its being attacked by rockets.

- These weaknesses resulted in part from inadequacies of preparedness and strategic and operative planning which go back long before the 2nd Lebanon war.

13. The decision made in the night of July 12th – to react (to the kidnapping) with immediate and substantive military action, and to set for it ambitious goals - limited Israel's range of options. In fact, after the initial decision had been made, Israel had only two main options, each with its coherent internal logic, and its set of costs and disadvantages. The first was a short, painful, strong and unexpected blow on Hezbollah, primarily through standoff fire-power. The second option was to bring about a significant change of the reality in the South of Lebanon with a large ground operation, including a temporary occupation of the South of Lebanon and 'cleaning' it of Hezbollah military infrastructure.

14.   The choice between these options was within the exclusive political discretion of the government; however, the way the original decision to go to war had been made; the fact Israel went to war before it decided which option to select, and without an exit strategy – all these constituted serious failures, which affected the whole war. Responsibility for these failures lay, as we had stressed in the Interim Report, on both the political and the military echelons.

15.   After the initial decision to use military force, and to the very end of the war, this period of 'equivocation' continued, with both the political and the military echelon not deciding between the two options: amplifying the military achievement by a broad military ground offensive, or abstaining from such a move and seeking to end the war quickly. This 'equivocation' did hurt Israel. Despite awareness of this fact, long weeks passed without a serious discussion of these options, and without a decision – one way or the other – between them.

16.   In addition to avoiding a decision about the trajectory of the military action, there was a very long delay in the deployment necessary for an extensive ground offensive, which was another factor limiting Israel's freedom of action and political flexibility: Till the first week of August, Israel did not prepare the military capacity to start a massive ground operation.

17.   As a result, Israel did not stop after its early military achievements, and was 'dragged' into a ground operation only after the political and diplomatic timetable prevented its effective completion. The responsibility for this basic failure in conducting the war lies at the doorstep of both the political and the military echelons.

18.   The overall image of the war was a result of a mixture of flawed conduct of the political and the military echelons and the interface between them, of flawed performance by the IDF, and especially the ground forces, and of deficient Israeli preparedness. Israel did not use its military force well and effectively, despite the fact that it was a limited war initiated by Israel itself. At the end of the day, Israel did not gain a political achievement because of military successes; rather, it relied on a political agreement, which included positive

elements for Israel, which permitted it to stop a war which it had failed to win.

19. This outcome was primarily caused by the fact that, from the very beginning, the war has not been conducted on the basis of deep understanding of the theatre of operations, of the IDF's readiness and preparedness, and of basic principles of using military power to achieve a political and diplomatic goal.

20. All in all, the IDF failed, especially because of the conduct of the high command and the ground forces, to provide an effective military response to the challenge posed to it by the war in Lebanon, and thus failed to provide the political echelon with a military achievement that could have served as the basis for political and diplomatic action. Responsibility for this outcomes lies mainly with the IDF, but the misfit between the mode of action and the goals determined by the political echelon share responsibility.

21. We should note that, alongside the failures in the IDF performance, there were also important military achievements. Special mention should go to the great willingness of the soldiers, especially reserve soldiers, to serve and fight in the war, as well as the many instances of heroism, courage, self-sacrifice and devotion of many commanders and soldiers.

22. The air force should be congratulated on very impressive achievements in this war. However, there were those in the IDF high command, joined by some in the political echelon, who entertained a baseless hope that the capabilities of the air force could prove decisive in the war. In fact, the impressive achievements of the air force were necessarily limited, and were eroded by the weaknesses in the overall performance of the IDF.

23. The "Hannit" episode colored to a large extent the whole performance of the Navy, despite the fact that it made a critical contribution to the naval blockade, and provided the Northern Command with varied effective support of its fighting.

24. We should also note that the war had significant diplomatic achievements. SC resolution 1701, and the fact it was adopted

unanimously, were an achievement for Israel. This conclusion stands even if it turns out that only a part of the stipulations of the resolution were implemented or will be implemented, and even if it could have been foreseen that some of them would not be implemented. This conclusion also does not depend on the intentions or goals of the powers that supported the resolution.

25.   We note, however, that we have seen no serious staff work on Israeli positions in the negotiations. This situation improved in part when the team headed by the prime minister's head of staff was established. The team worked efficiently and with dedication, professionalism and coordination. This could not compensate, however, for the absence of preparatory staff work and discussions in the senior political echelon.

26.   This fact may have much significance to the way Israel conducts negotiations, and to the actual content of the arrangements reached. In such negotiations, decisions are often made that may have far-reaching implications on Israel's interests, including the setting of precedents.

27.   The staff work done in the Ministry of Foreign Affairs concerning the adoption of a favorable resolution in the Security Council was, in the main, quick, systematic and efficient. At the same time, for a variety of reasons, it did not reflect clear awareness of the essential need to maintain an effective relationship between military achievements and diplomatic activities.

28.   We now turn to the political and military activity concerning the ground operation at the end of the war. This is one of the central foci of public debate.

29.   True, in hindsight, the large ground operation did not achieve its goals of limiting the rocket fire and changing the picture of the war. It is not clear what the ground operation contributed to speeding up the diplomatic achievement or improving it. It is also unclear to what extent starting the ground offensive affected the reactions of the government of Lebanon and Hezbollah to the ceasefire.

30. Nonetheless, it is important to stress that the evaluation of these decisions should not be made with hindsight. It cannot depend on the achievements or the costs these decisions in fact had. The evaluation must be based only on the reasons for the operation, and its risks and prospects as they were known - or as they should have been known - when it was decided upon. Moreover, it is impossible to evaluate the ground operation at the end of the war without recalling the developments that preceded it and the repeated delays in the adoption of the Security Council resolution; and as a part of the overall conduct of the war.

31. Against this background, we make the following findings on the main decisions:

   • The cabinet decision of August 9th – to approve in principle the IDF plan, but to authorize the PM and the MOD to decide if and when it should be activated, according to the diplomatic timetable - was almost inevitable, giving the Israeli government necessary military and political flexibility.

   • The decision to start in fact the ground operation was within the political and professional discretion of its makers, on the basis of the facts before them. The goals of the ground operation were legitimate, and were not exhausted by the wish to hasten or improve the diplomatic achievement. There was no failure in that decision in itself, despite its limited achievements and its painful costs.

   • Both the position of the Prime minister – who had preferred to avoid the ground operation – and the position of the Minister of Defense – who had thought it would have served Israel's interest to go for it – had been taken on the merits and on the basis of evidence. Both enjoyed serious support among the members of the general staff of the IDF and others. Even if both statesmen took into account political and public concerns – a fact we cannot ascertain - we believe that they both acted out of a strong and sincere perception of what they thought at the time was Israel's interest.

32.   We want to stress: The duty to make these difficult decisions was the political leaders'. The sole test of these decisions is public and political.

33.   At the same time, we also note that:

- We have not found within either the political or the military echelons a serious consideration of the question whether it was reasonable to expect military achievements in 60 hours that could have contributed meaningfully to any of the goals of the operation;

- We have not found that the political echelon was aware of the details of the fighting in real time, and we have not seen a discussion, in either the political or the military echelons, of the issue of stopping the military operation after the Security Council resolution was adopted;

- We have not seen an explanation of the tension between the great effort to get additional time to conclude the first stage of the planned ground operation and the decisions not to go on fighting until the ceasefire itself.

34.   A description of failures in the conduct of war may be regarded as harming Israel. There will be those who may use our findings to hurt Israel and its army. We nonetheless point out these failures and shortcomings because we are certain that only in this way Israel may come out of this ordeal strengthened. We are pleased that processes of repair have already started. We recommend a deep and systematic continuation of such processes. It is exclusively in the hands of Israeli leaders and public to determine whether, when facing challenges in the future, we will come to them more prepared and ready, and whether we shall cope with them in a more serious and responsible way than the way the decision-makers had acted – in the political and the military echelons -- in the 2nd Lebanon war.

35.   Our recommendations contain suggestions for systemic and deep changes in the modalities of thinking and acting of the political and military echelons and their interface, in both routine and emergency, including war. These are deep and

critical processes. Their significance should not be obscured by current affairs, local successes or initial repairs. A persistent and prolonged effort, on many levels, will be needed in order to bring about the essential improvements in the ways of thinking and acting of the political-military systems.

36.   For these reasons we would like to caution against dangers which might upset plans and delay required change processes, and thus produce dangerous results:

- Fear of criticism in case of failure may lead to defensive reactions, working by the book, and abstention from making resolute decisions and preferring non-action. Such behavior is undesirable and also dangerous.

- In a dynamic complex reality, one should not prepare better for the last war. It is also essential not to limit oneself to superficial action, designed to create an appearance that flaws had been corrected.

- It is also essential not to focus exclusively on coping with dangers, but to combine readiness for threat scenarios with an active seeking of opportunities.

- When speaking on learning, one should take into account that enemies, too, are learning their lessons.

37.   The 2nd Lebanon War has brought again to the foreground for thought and discussion issues that some parts of Israeli society had preferred to suppress: Israel cannot survive in this region, and cannot live in it in peace or at least non-war, unless people in Israel itself and in its surroundings believe that Israel has the political and military leadership, military capabilities, and social robustness that will allow her to deter those of its neighbors who wish to harm her, and to prevent them - if necessary through the use of military force - from achieving their goal.

38.   These truths do not depend on one's partisan or political views. Israel must - politically and morally - seek peace with its neighbors and make necessary compromises. At the same time, seeking peace or managing the conflict must come from

a position of social, political and military strength, and through the ability and willingness to fight for the state, its values and the security of its population even in the absence of peace.

39.   These truths have profound and far-reaching implications for many dimensions of life in Israel and the ways its challenges are managed. Beyond examining the way the Lebanon War was planned and conducted; beyond the examination of flaws in decision-making and performance that had been revealed in it - important as they may be; these are the central questions that the Lebanon war has raised. These are issues that lie at the very essence of our existence here as a Jewish and democratic state. These are the questions we need to concentrate on.

40.   We hope that our findings and conclusions in the Interim and the Final Reports will bring about not only a redress of failings and flaws, but help Israeli society, its leaders and thinkers, to advance the long-term goals of Israel, and develop the appropriate ways to address the challenges and respond to them.

41.   We are grateful for the trust put in us when this difficult task was given to us. If we succeed in facilitating rectification of the failings we have identified - this will be our best reward.

Thank you.

	Appendix B Hizballah Rockets*		
System	Range (Kilometers)	Warhead Weight (Kilograms)	Supplier
ZelZal-2	210	600	Iran
Nazeat	100-140	1,300(6)/250(10)	Iran
Fajr 3	43	45	Iran
Fajr 5	75	90	Iran
302mm	75	100	Syria
220mm	70	Unknown	Syria
122mm	20	30	Iran/Syria
107mm	6	Unknown	Iran/Syria

*Makovsky, David and White, Jeffrey. "Lessons and Implications of the Israel Hizballah War." *The Washington Institute for Near East Policy*. Policy Focus #60, October 2006.

Appendix C
Reported Hizballah Antitank Weapons*

System	Range (Kilometers)	Penetration	Guidance System (Manual/Laser/Wire)
Kornet AT–14	3.5 mi	1,100–1,200 mm	Laser
Kornet AT–5	75 m	800 mm	Wire
Metis-M AT–13	80 m to 1.5 km	460–850 mm	Wire
Sagger AT–3	3 km	200 mm	Wire
Fagot AT–4	70 m to 2 km	400 mm	Wire
Milan	400–2,000 m	352 mm	Wire
TOW	600–3,700 m	800 mm	Wire
RPG–29	460 m	750 mm	Manual
RPG–7	500 m	3300 mm	Manual

*Makovsky, David and White, Jeffrey. "Lessons and Implications of the Israel Hizballah War." *The Washington Institute for Near East Policy*. Policy Focus #60, October 2006.

Appendix D

The following is a chronological list of events along Israel's northern border in which Israeli civilians or soldiers were killed or wounded from May 2000 until 12 July 2006.*

27 May 2006 - An IDF soldier was wounded when Katyushas were fired at an army base at Mt. Meron in the upper Galilee.

27 December 2005 - A branch of a Palestinian organization connected to Al-Qaida fired six Katyushas, damaging a house in Kiryat Shmona and a house in Metulla. In response, the IAF attacked a training base of the Popular Front, south of Beirut.

21 November 2005 - An attempt to kidnap an IDF soldier was foiled when paratroopers patrolling near Rajar village discerned a Hizbullah unit approaching. Private David Markovitz opened fire, killing all four. In a heavy attack of mortars and Katyusha rockets that ensued, nine soldiers and and two civilians were injured.

29 June 2005 - More than 20 mortars were fired from across the border. Cpl. Uzi Peretz of the Golani Brigade was killed and four soldiers wounded, including the unit's doctor. Fire was exchanged and helicopters and planes attacked five Hizbullah outposts in the Reches Ramim area.

7 April 2005 - Two Israeli Arabs from the village of Rajar on the Israel-Lebanon border were kidnapped by Hizbullah operatives and held in captivity for four days in an attempt to obtain information on Israel.

9 January 2005 - An explosive device was detonated against an IDF patrol at Nahal Sion. One Israeli soldier was killed, and a UN officer was killed.

20 July 2004 - Hizbullah sniper fired at an IDF post in the western sector of the Israeli-Lebanese border. Two IDF soldiers were killed.

7 May 2004 - Fire in the Mt. Dov sector. IDF soldier Dennis Leminov was killed, and two other soldiers were severely wounded. The IDF returned fire.

19 January 2004 - An antitank missile was fired at IDF D9 while neutralizing explosive charges near Zari't. An IDF soldier, Yan Rotzenski, was killed and another soldier was severely wounded.

---

*"Hizbullah Attacks Along Israel's Northern Border May 2000–June 2006," *Israel Ministry of Foreign Affairs*, http://www.mfa.gov.il/NR/exeres/9EE216D7-82EF-4274-B80D-6BBD1803E8A7,framcless.htm?NRMODE=Published (accessed 20 August 2007).

6 October 2003 - Staff Sgt. David Solomonov was killed when Hizbullah fired at an IDF force south of the Fatma Gate in the eastern sector. In addition, the Hizbullah fired missiles and rockets at an IDF post in the Reches Ramim area.

10 August 2003 - Haviv Dadon, 16, of Shlomi, was struck in the chest and killed by shrapnel from an antiaircraft shell fired by Hizbullah terrorists in Lebanon. Four others were wounded.

20 July 2003 - Hizbullah snipers fired on an Israeli outpost near Shtula, killing two Israeli soldiers.

7 May 2003 - Hizbullah attacked IDF positions in the Sheba farms with heavy rocket, mortar, and small arms fire. One Israeli soldier was killed and five others were wounded in the attack.

29 August 2002 - Fire at an IDF post in the Mt. Dov sector. IDF soldier Ofer Misali was killed, and two other soldiers were lightly wounded.

12 March 2002 - Infiltration: In a shooting attack on the Shlomi- Metzuba route. Six Israelis civilians were killed, among them IDF officer Lt. German Rojkov.

14 April 2001 - Fire at an IDF post in the Mt. Dov sector. IDF soldier Elad Litvak was killed.

16 February 2001 - Fire at an IDF convoy on Mt. Dov. IDF soldier Elad Shneor was killed, and three other soldiers were wounded.

26 November 2000 - A charge was detonated near an IDF convoy. IDF soldier Khalil Taher was killed and two other soldiers were wounded.

7 October 2000 - Kidnapping: Three IDF soldiers: Adi Avitan, Omer Soued and Binyamin Avraham were kidnapped by the Hizballah from the Mt. Dov sector.

In addition, Hizbullah was involved in terrorist acts carried out by affiliated Palestinian terrorist cells in Israel:

28 April 2001 - A 60-year-old Israeli man was found stabbed to death in Kfar Ba'aneh, near Carmiel in Galilee. The terrorists responsible for the attack were apprehended in July. Six members of a Hizbullah-linked Palestinian terrorist cell responsible for the murder were arrested in July. The murder was the initiation rite of the organization.

1 April 2001 - A 42-year-old Israeli woman was stabbed to death in Haifa. Her murder was the initiation rite of a terrorist cell, whose members were apprehended in July. Six members of a Hizbullah-linked Palestinian terrorist cell responsible for the murder, originally thought to be criminally motivated, were arrested in July. The murder was the initiation rite of one of the terrorists into the organization.

About the Author

Matt M. Matthews joined the Combat Studies Institute (CSI) in July 2005 after working for 16 years as a member of the World Class Opposing Force (OPFOR) for the Battle Command Training Program at Fort Leavenworth, Kansas. Mr. Matthews graduated from Kansas State University in 1986 with a BS in History. He served as an Infantry enlisted man in the Regular Army from 1977 to 1981, a Cavalry officer in the US Army Reserve from 1983 to 1986, and an Armor officer in the Kansas Army National Guard from 1986 to 1991. Mr. Matthews is the author of CSI Press publications *The Posse Comitatus Act* and the *United States Army: A Historical Perspective and Operation AL FAJR: A Study in Army and Marine Corps Joint Operations* and *The US Army on the Mexican Border: A Historical Perspective*. He has coauthored numerous scholarly articles on the Civil War in the Trans-Mississippi, including "Shot All to Pieces: The Battle of Lone Jack," "To Play a Bold Game: The Battle of Honey Springs," and "Better Off in Hell: The Evolution of the Kansas Red Legs." He is a frequent speaker at Civil War Roundtables, and he recently appeared on the History Channel as a historian for Bill Kurtis' Investigating History. Mr. Matthews was the mayor of Ottawa, Kansas.